HERCULES

BERNARD EVSLIN

HERCULES

ILLUSTRATED BY JOS. A. SMITH

WILLIAM MORROW AND COMPANY
NEW YORK • 1984

1 2 3 4 5 6 7 8 9 10

Library of Congress Cataloging in Publication Data
Evslin, Bernard. Hercules.
Summary: Retells the adventures of the demigod Hercules as he struggles to
accomplish seemingly impossible tasks. 1. Hercules (Roman mythology)—Juvenile
literature. [1. Hercules (Roman mythology) 2. Mythology, Roman]
I. Title. BL820.H5E97 1984   292′.211   83-23834
ISBN 0-688-02748-2 (reinforced trade ed.)

FOR GALEAL
eldest grandson and youngest reader

Those in the Book

CONTENTS

HERCULES

THE TWINS

ONE MORNING, LONG LONG AGO, WHEN THE WORLD WAS new, all the bells in Thebes rang at once. People rushed out of their houses, shouting and laughing, and began to dance in the streets of the marble city. For the bells were announcing that their tall beautiful princess had given birth to a boy. The old king and the prince and all the court paraded to the temple to thank Zeus for their new little prince.

Suddenly, the bells stopped ringing. People stopped dancing. A terrible whisper sped from mouth to ear. The princess was still in labor; another baby was coming.

Why was this such dreadful news? What's wrong with twins? Everything—if they're both heirs to a kingdom. This had happened before in another country close by. Both twins had claimed the crown, starting a bloody civil war.

So Prince Amphitryon stayed in the temple after the others had left. He stretched his arms to the altar and prayed that the second twin would be a girl.

A messenger rushed up the temple steps just as the prince was coming down. The man fell on his knees, stuttering, so frightened he could hardly speak. And the prince knew that his wife had given birth to a second son and that the messenger was afraid of being killed on the spot for bringing bad news.

But Amphitryon, who was very fierce in battle, was a kindly man at heart. He dismissed the messenger and walked slowly back to the castle. Since he was a real leader who did everything possible to drive fear from the hearts of his people, he forced himself to smile as he passed through the crowd. He waved cheerfully, as if he had received the best news in the world. Seeing him this way, the people cast off their gloom and milled about the streets again.

He was still trying his best to look cheerful when he entered the chamber of the princess—where he received another surprise. One baby was three times as big as his brother and different in other ways. He wasn't bald and squinched and squally like most infants, but had a nimbus of red-gold hair and huge gray eyes and lay there smiling to himself. The prince looked at him in wonder. The princess was radiant! She was brimming with joy. Seeing this, the prince stopped pretending; his joy became real. He swept Alcmene into his arms, and, since she was holding the twins, they were all in his arms, his wife and his two sons.

"We need another name!" cried Alcmene. "Hurry, think of one!"

2

HERCULES

The name they had already chosen was *Iphicles,* after a great-grandfather. And this they gave to the smaller twin, who had been born first.

"Oh, let us think of something splendid for the other one," said Alcmene. "No ordinary name will do."

They thought and thought, and finally named the larger twin *Hercules,* which means "earth's glory."

When they went out on the balcony that sunset to face the cheering mob, and Amphitryon held first one boy, then the other, into the red light of the falling sun, the people thought the names had been well chosen. And another whisper began to pass from mouth to ear. "That big one—he looks like he's six months old. That's no mortal child. His father must be a god."

They meant to praise their new prince, but, as it happened, this was the worst thing they could have said. These words were to plunge young Hercules into dangers that no one had ever faced before, making him fight for his life against the most fearsome beasts and monsters and demons in that terrible magical world of long ago.

THE SERPENTS

THE ANCIENT WORLD WAS LIKE OURS IN SOME WAYS; there were always plenty of busybodies ready to pass on gossip, especially if it might cause trouble. And word soon came to Hera, queen of the gods, about what was being whispered in Thebes. "That son of Princess Alcmene . . . he's too big and beautiful for mortal child. He must be the son of a god."

And jealous Hera immediately decided that this wonderful child's father must be her own husband, Zeus. For, as king of the gods, he had always felt free to take as many wives as he liked. When she accused him of being Hercules' father, he denied it; but she didn't believe him. And as more and more tales came to her of how big and strong and brave the boy was growing, she decided to kill him.

"My brother Poseidon owes me a favor," she said to herself. "I'll get him to lend me a sea serpent or two."

As it happened, that afternoon, Alcmene had told the boys' nurse to take them into the castle garden to play. They crawled about the edge of the flower beds awhile and played with pebbles and pine cones, Iphicles always grabbing whatever his brother had. For he was a greedy, aggressive child, while Hercules, although so much bigger, was very gentle. He seemed to know that he had to be careful not to use his strength against his little twin.

The children were sleepy, and the nurse put them into their bull-hide cradles that were slung side by side between two trees. They slept. The cradles swung softly in the wind. Then something crawled into Hercules' sleep. He smiled. He didn't know what a dream was and thought everything he saw was real, sleeping or waking. And this worm was very handsome, not pink and slimy, but seeming to be made of hard smooth leather, blue and green, the colors melting into each other like water when the sun shines on it. What's more, the worm was growing very fast, sprouting out of itself. It was as big as he was and growing longer as he watched.

He opened his eyes. There, curled around the trunk of the tree, and stretching over the cradle to look down into his face, was a huge serpent. It unwrapped itself from the tree and slithered into the bull-hide cradle, rearing up from its own coils and dipping its wedge-shaped head to look at him out of flat black eyes.

Hercules smiled. He thought it was a big worm. He reached up to pat its face. The coils shifted and more snake came out and cast a loop about his waist. Hercules thought the snake was hugging him and gurgled with joy. The loop tightened. The snake was hugging him tightly, too tightly. He could hardly breathe.

Then he heard his brother screaming. Another serpent had come into the other cradle and was wrapping itself around his little twin.

Now, a child always finds it very hard to understand the first cruel thing that happens, and Hercules had been treated with great love and kindness by his mother, his father, his nurse, and everyone in the castle. So although his breath was being squeezed out of him, and his ribs were about to crack, he didn't understand that evil had come into his life, that someone's jealous hatred had taken the form of a serpent that was trying to kill him. He couldn't realize it; he was much too young. His breath was like fire in his lungs, and the loops were squeezing tighter and tighter.

Then his brother's scream pierced the fog.

That scream was pure fear. It was a cry of terrified pain, and, coming from someone else, it made the fighting blood boil up in little Hercules for the first time; powers that had been sleeping in him began to awaken.

He drew a big breath, deep, deep. At first, the pain grew worse, because deep breathing made the coils tighter. But he tried to ignore the pain and kept drawing more air into his lungs. He felt the coils loosen a bit, enough for him to slip his hand out and grasp the serpent under the head. Then he began to squeeze.

Iphicles was still screaming. And that screaming, that terror, that pain, made Hercules' hand grow tighter and tighter. He felt the coils loosen as the snake began to strangle.

Still not quite knowing what he was doing, he

climbed to his feet, balancing himself on the swinging cradle, and leaped into his brother's cradle. Iphicles' head was lolling now; the child had fainted. With his other hand, Hercules seized the serpent that was throttling his brother—caught it under the head in the same terrible grip—and began to squeeze. And thinking that his brother was badly hurt, a wild grief made his left hand tighten and tighten, squeezing the breath out of this second snake.

The loops fell away from Iphicles, and young Hercules crouched in the cradle holding both serpents. He didn't want to kill them; he had never killed anything. But they couldn't live either. They were too evil. So he braided them about each other and tossed them out of the cradle. They fell to the ground still wound around each other. And the braided serpents, trying to untangle themselves, choked each other to death.

When the nurse ran up, shrieking, followed by the gardeners, followed by other servants of the castle, they saw two huge dead sea serpents still wound about each other. A curious bellowing sound came down out of the tree. They looked up and there in the cradle they saw the young Hercules, holding his brother in his arms, sobbing, trying to wake him up.

Iphicles had three broken ribs. The best healers were called to the castle. And the child came of strong warrior stock. He slowly mended, although forever afterward, he was afraid of snakes. As for young Hercules, his body was blotched with black and purple bruises, but the springy keg of his ribs was unhurt.

However, the child had changed. He seemed to have grown another six inches since his battle with the serpents. He was less a baby now, more a little boy. Nor did he always smile now. Sometimes his face would grow solemn, and a tiny furrow would come between his gray eyes. And his mother knew the child was trying to understand the evil that had come crawling into his life, and that he couldn't do it. She was very proud of him and loved him more than ever, and so did his father. But they felt grief mixing with their pride. For dimly they knew that this child was truly different in some marvelous dangerous way, and that the difference was making him the target of some unknown wickedness—something more fearsome than a human enemy, something full of mysterious strength and surprise. They also knew that there was nothing much they could do to help their child except try to prepare him for what he would have to face.

Indeed, when Hera learned what had happened to the serpents she had sent, she was more certain than ever that the Theban gossip was true: that Hercules was the son of a god and that that god was Zeus. And her jealous fury grew and grew.

"How could a baby do that?" she said to herself. "Is Zeus shielding him in some magical way? Yes. He must be. But I've outwitted Zeus before, and I'll do it again. I'll get rid of that overgrown brat if it's the last thing I do."

CHIRON

GGGGGGGGGGGGGGGGGGGGGGGGG

THE GODS GO BY A DIFFERENT TIME. EVERYTHING IS larger for them. Their days are our years. So, while Hera did not forget Hercules, she had other grudges to settle. And when she turned her attention to him again a few weeks later—in her time—he was almost sixteen years old, an enormous youth, bigger and stronger than any man in Thebes and still growing.

He did not live at home with his parents and his brother but in the wild hills of Thessaly where he was being tutored by a very wise creature named Chiron, who was only half man, the other half being horse. That is, he had a horse's body up to the neck, but from that body sprouted the chest, head, and arms of a man. The tribe he belonged to was called the centaurs. They too were hated by Hera, who, indeed, had made them become the way they were.

Long before, Zeus had happened to admire a beauti-

11

ful maiden of Thessaly and had been unwise enough to let Hera know. "Look at her," he said one day. "Down there in Thessaly—that girl running through the fields. Isn't she lovely? So long-legged and graceful, just like a filly . . ."

Whereupon Hera cast a curse, saying, "Miserable girl, you shall become more like a filly than you wish." She said it under her breath so Zeus wouldn't hear. But curses, like prayers, don't have to be said loudly if you mean them, and as soon as Hera had said this, the girl found herself running through the fields more swiftly than ever because she now had the body of a filly. Later, she became the mother of the tribe called centaurs.

But Zeus, pitying her and angry at what Hera had done, tried to turn the curse into a blessing. He gave the centaurs happy reckless natures, filling them with a love of wild places, and a special wisdom about trees and plants and animals.

And it was Chiron, wisest of all the centaurs, who became tutor to the young Hercules. The boy spent happy years with him in the hills of Thessaly.

Chiron taught him the ways of birds and beasts and of all the creatures who dwell in the mountain lakes and the swift little rivers. Taught him to read the weather in the dance of leaves and the flight of birds, and how to sniff the wind for rain. Taught him how to take honey from the hive without offending the bees, where to find nuts and berries, and which mushrooms were good to eat and which were poison. Wandering the woods and fields with Chiron, young Hercules learned how certain herbs cure fever and how to crush wild oregano leaves

to make a paste that will stop bleeding. And how to pack a wound with spider web and moldy bread to make it heal clean. All very useful lore for someone who is going to have to do a great deal of fighting.

For sport, Hercules raced and wrestled the young centaurs. He lost the races, for they could run more swiftly than horses, but he always won the wrestling matches and finally had to give them up because he had become too strong even for the powerful young centaurs. But he loved to wrestle and roamed the woods looking for bears. He grew very fond of the big furry animals because they enjoyed wrestling as much as he did, and he didn't have to worry about hurting them. But he kept growing and got stronger every day; he realized that the time was coming when he wouldn't even be able to wrestle bears. He had no way of knowing that this magically happy time in the hills of Thessaly was to end so suddenly.

For Hera had been thinking again about Hercules and was planning what to do. But this time, she planned more carefully.

THE VISION

"I'LL HAVE TO GO SLOWLY," SAID HERA TO HERSELF. "Zeus has made me promise not to harm any of his sons or daughters. I mean to break that promise, of course, but I don't want to be caught. So, I can't simply kill Hercules—who's very hard to kill, anyway. I'll have to trick him into arranging his own doom. Yes-s-s . . . I'll make him use his powers against himself. He's warm-hearted, hot-tempered, blazing with energy. And if I can't use his own heat to burn him out, my name's not Hera."

One hot afternoon in May, Hercules lay in a field of flowering clover. The clover smell hung sweet as honey, and bees were among the blossoms; their humming made the world's drowsiest sound. Hera appeared. She stood looking down at him. She seemed tall as a tree and was clad in purple, a golden crown on her head.

"Are you a goddess?" he murmured.

15

"I am Hera, queen of the gods."

"Am I dreaming?"

"It doesn't matter. I am real."

He stared at her.

"Hercules, behold—"

She faded, and a picture branded itself on the golden air where she had stood. The people in the picture moved and had voices, and everything they did and said was terribly important. If it was a dream, it was the kind that seems realer than life. Hercules saw himself standing. He was a man now, with a golden beard. He wore a lion skin and carried a club and was much bigger than the youth lying on the grass. And this man, whom Hercules recognized as himself grown-up, was waiting for someone.

A woman walked toward him; it was his wife, and she held the hands of two children, a boy and a girl. Hercules knew that they were his children because they looked like him. Then the youth on the grass was horrified to see the man lift his club and smash it down on the woman's head. She fell. The children screamed and ran away. The man caught them in two strides, dropped his club, lifted a child in each hand, and knocked their heads together. The heads split like eggs. He dropped the dead children on their dead mother, raised his face to the sky, and howled like a wolf. Then he rushed off among the trees.

The bodies disappeared. Hera stood there looking down at him. There was such a tearing grief in the youth's heart that he couldn't look at the goddess. He knelt on the grass covering his face with his hands.

"Look at me."

16

He dropped his hands. Her face was very stern.

"I have come to do you a great service, to show you the man you will be," said Hera. "You know now what he will do."

"Why did he kill them?"

"Not *he,* you. That was *you.* You recognized yourself."

"Yes . . ."

"You have seen yourself married, with two lovely innocent children. In a fit of madness, you shall kill them. All, all."

"Why?"

"In madness there is no 'why.' "

"I don't believe it. It's a false vision. It won't happen."

"Hercules, the matter is too important for you to lie to yourself. You know there is truth in that vision. Search your heart, and you will find wrath and evil at the bottom of it."

"It won't happen."

"Oh, yes it will."

"It won't! I'll kill myself now, and it can't happen."

"I have come to save you. I am your friend. You don't have to kill yourself. I shall show you a way you can cleanse your soul of these wicked impulses. You can so purify yourself that it will become impossible for you to commit such a murder."

"How? How? Tell me!"

"There is only one way, and you must follow my instructions exactly. You must go to the king of Mycenae, King Eurystheus, and put yourself under his orders. Twelve years you must serve him, and whatever he tells you to do, you must do. If you faithfully carry out his wishes, without argument and without hesitation, you shall cleanse yourself of evil, and the foul vision you have seen today shall remain a dream."

"Must I go to Mycenae now?"

"Now. Don't wait to say farewell to Chiron. Do not go back to Thebes to bid your mother and father goodby, nor to see your brother. Leave this place immediately and go straight to Mycenae. The king is waiting."

She vanished.

Hercules arose from the grass and looked about. He couldn't believe that this was the same sunny slope, that this was the same bed of clover, and these the same bees. Everything was changed. The grass was charred; the bees were tiny demons; and the flowers stank of blood. He couldn't bear to leave without embracing Chiron once more. But he didn't dare disobey Hera. Weeping bitterly, he left that place where he had been so happy. He didn't exactly know where Mycenae was, but he was sure he would find it before he wanted to.

THE TASKMASTER

HERA HAD SEARCHED ALL THE LANDS OF THE MIDDLE
Sea for a king stupid enough and cowardly enough to
carry out her evil wishes and enjoy doing it. She found
him in Mycenae. King Eurystheus was a brutal, pig-
faced man who took great pleasure in causing pain,
especially if he could do it without any risk.

Hera appeared to him and told him that he was to be
given the gift of a young slave, who was the world's
strongest man and would obey all the king's commands.

"If he's so strong, why should he do what anyone tells
him?" said Eurystheus.

"He is under a curse, and this is the way he must
work it off. He will try to do any task you set him. If he
fails, he dies, and I shall reward you for causing his
death."

"Suppose he succeeds?"

"He won't. But if he does, you will get the credit for

his deeds, and everyone will say you are a wise and powerful king."

"I am! I am!" cried Eurystheus. "I must be very wise and powerful, because soon I am to have the strongest man in the world to serve me. What's his first task?"

"He is to hunt the Nemean Lion and bring you its hide."

"The Nemean Lion! Nobody can kill that monster. The best hunters in the world have gone against him and been devoured."

"Yes," said Hera. "I know."

And vanished.

THE NEMEAN LION

AS THE KING WAITED FOR HERCULES TO COME TO HIS castle, he grew more and more frightened. Despite what Hera had said, he couldn't imagine the strongest man in the world taking orders from anyone. He kept thinking what this young giant might do if he got angry, what might happen when Hercules heard him say, "Go hunt the Nemean Lion. Bring me its hide." He pictured how a huge hand would come down at him, grab him by the back of the neck, snatch him off the throne, and hold him dangling like a kitten. *Himself,* Eurystheus, the king! Perhaps the hand would slap him a few times as he dangled there. Maybe do worse. And all the people would know him for what he was: not a stern powerful ruler, but a coward. And the more he thought about Hercules, the more frightened he grew.

Finally, the day came.

The king had posted lookouts beyond the city walls.

23

Now a messenger rushed into the throne room, crying, "He's coming! He's coming! And oh, your majesty, he's a giant!"

Although it was a hot day, the king crouched on his throne, shaking and quaking as though he were sitting in a tub of ice water.

"No," he said to himself. "I'm not going to meet that brute. Why should I? What's the use of being a king if I can't make somebody else do dangerous things for me? I'll send Copreus to meet him. Let Copreus tell him about the lion. And if Hera is right, the lion will eat him up, and I'll never have to worry again."

Mycenae was a walled city. Its walls were tall and thick, made of heavy stone slabs. The only way in was through an enormous iron gate. But when Hercules reached the city, this gate was closed. He didn't know what to do. Hera had said he must report to the king, and the king would be expecting him. But the gate was bolted.

He felt himself growing angry. He felt his hands opening and closing, and the muscles of his back and shoulders filling with wild strength. The city was locked against him, but chains and bolts wouldn't mean much if he simply tore the iron gate from its hinges and hurled it away. But before he could touch it, he heard voices shouting, "In the name of the king! In the name of the king!" He dropped his arms. Through the gate he saw guards trotting toward the wall. They wore brass armor and brass helmets and carried spears. They reached the gate, unbolted it, and came through. They stood in double file facing him. Hercules started toward the open gate.

24

"Halt!" said a voice.

A little plump man came through the file of soldiers. He wore a white tunic and bore a white herald's staff.

"Close it!"

Hercules saw six soldiers swing the gate shut. The little man turned to face him. "Are you Hercules?"

"I am. Why do you close the gate against me?"

"King's orders."

"But it is him I have come to see."

"I speak for the king. Your business is with me."

"What is your name, good herald?"

"I am Copreus."

Hercules shouted with laughter, for the word means "dung man," or someone who does dirty jobs. He saw the man flush bright red, and he stopped laughing because he knew it was rude, and Chiron had taught him always to be courteous.

"I am proud of my name," said the herald stiffly. "It means that I serve the king by doing things he finds unpleasant."

"Good sir, I apologize. I did not mean to hurt your feelings. But why should the king find it so unpleasant to speak to me?"

"Because he is tenderhearted. It makes him sad to send a young man to his death."

"Am I being sent to my death?"

"To hunt the Nemean Lion. It comes to the same thing."

"Will you take a message back to the king?"

"Yes."

"Tell him that I shall take every care not to sadden him with the news of my death. Tell him that I go to

25

hunt the lion and that I shall return with its hide. And when I do, I hope to be able to thank him personally for giving me the chance to perform so splendid a deed."

"Brave words, my lad. Do you know anything about this beast whose hide you mean to take?"

"No, sir. It's a lion like any other, I presume."

"It's a lion *unlike* any other. Its parents were Typhon and Ekidne. Typhon, you know, was a monster out of the First Days, so huge and fierce that no one could believe such a creature could exist. But he did, he did . . . He was as tall as a cedar; his head was a donkey's head. His legs were enormous serpents. Instead of hands, a dragon head sprouted from each wrist, belching flame. His strength was the strength of an avalanche, a hurricane, a tidal wave. The gods themselves, they say, were afraid of Typhon; they shuddered on Olympus when he passed below, and hid in a cave until he went away. He, Typhon, was the father of your Nemean Lion. And the lion's mother was a female monster named Ekidne. She was half woman, half snake, and the halves changed places. That is, sometimes her body was a woman's and her head was a snake's, and when she got tired of herself that way, she put on a snake's body and a woman's head . . . and was equally ugly both ways. In fact, Typhon was the ugliest male in the first days of the world, and Ekidne was the ugliest female. They were so hideous that every other creature fled them, and they were left with each other. So they married, and Ekidne had a litter of monsters. And the youngest of the litter, and some say the worst, was the Nemean Lion. A lion, yes, but bigger than an elephant, its teeth like ivory daggers, its claws like brass hooks, and its hide like armor, which no weapon can pierce. That is the Nemean Lion, which keeps the whole country between Corinth and Argos in utter terror and has killed and eaten a generation of fighting men."

"Well, gentle Copreus, I thank you for the information. It's always good to know the worst about your enemy; then you won't have any unpleasant surprises."

"Good hunting," said Copreus.

"Thank you again. And my best wishes to your royal master."

Hercules turned and loped off. Everyone stared after him in amazement.

Hercules had learned archery from the centaurs, who did it differently from ordinary men. Bowmen of the time used short bows and drew the string only to their chest. But the centaurs were so long-armed and powerful that they were able to use an enormous bow made of ash strengthened by stag horn; their arrows were as long as spears. When a centaur notched an arrow, he drew the bowstring back past his shoulder, bending the bow almost double, shooting the arrow with terrific force. And the young Hercules was soon outshooting his teachers. He was able to send his bolts through a stone wall three feet thick.

He carried that bow now as he started for Nemea to hunt the lion. But he had no spear. He knew he would have to make his own, for ordinary spears were too small for him. He searched the river shore until he found an old boat, half-covered by reeds. Its hull was smashed in, but its mast was still good. He broke the mast off; that was his spear shaft. He didn't want to use a leaf-shaped spearhead, which made a large wound. He

27

needed something with a needle point if he was to have any chance of piercing the lion's armor hide. He found an old iron spike and drove it into the end of the mast. Then he sharpened the spike against a rock, flaking the rust away, until it was needle-sharp. As he went along, he practiced throwing the spear at trees and didn't stop until he split an oak with a single cast.

But he wasn't satisfied even then. "With my centaur bow, I can shoot an arrow through a stone wall," he said to himself. "And split an oak tree with my new spear. But it seems I'm to meet some very terrible creatures, beginning with this lion, and, if I'm not lucky, ending with this lion. I'm quite large for a person, it's true, but these monsters make me seem the size of a mouse. So I can't depend on strength alone. No, I'll need cleverness and speed." And thinking about how swift he would have to become, he began to run. He ran as fast as he could, then faster yet. He found himself running so fast, and enjoying the speed so much, that he didn't want to stop even when he saw the wall of a ruined temple looming up before him. He rushed at the wall, planted the butt of his huge spear on the ground, and vaulted. He hurled himself up, up. The mast bent under his weight, then sprang up. He stretched his arms and flattened his body and rode the springing shaft over the wall.

Once he discovered vaulting, he couldn't stop. He kept running. He vaulted rivers and huts. He loved it. It was like flying. He was enjoying himself so much that he was surprised when he saw a river, and beyond the river, a mountain and knew that it must be Mount Nemea, where the lion hunted.

The sun was sinking. The mountain threw a blue

shadow. "This is the right time of day," he thought. "Lions hunt early and kill before evening. He will be heavy with food now, and perhaps a little slower. Who knows?"

He heard something roar. A savage deafening roar. "I was wrong," thought Hercules. "He still sounds hungry." He crouched behind a rock, waiting for the lion.

Then he saw it come. Smoothly, heavily, it came. Its hide was yellow and its mane was black; its teeth were a deadly white grin. He couldn't believe its size. It was as big as an elephant. It roared again, and the shattering sound was like being hit by a club. It came on and on: pure yellow murder.

Hercules took an arrow from his quiver and put it to his bowstring. The huge bow bent double as he drew the arrow back past his ear, past his shoulder. He held the bow bent, waiting for the lion to come closer, then loosed the arrow. It sang through the air, struck the lion's shoulder, and glanced off, without leaving a scratch. Fast as he could move, he snatched arrows from his quiver and shot them. One by one he saw them skid off the beast. The lion shook its great head and yawned. Hercules could see its ivory teeth glinting and between them the black hole of its gullet looking like the mouth of a cave big enough to swallow him, his bow and arrows, and the rock he was hiding behind.

He tossed his bow away, drew back his spear, and hurled it with all his might. It skidded off the lion's head and split a tree. The lion looked after the spear, swiveled its head, and looked toward the man. It prowled closer, so close that Hercules gagged on the rotten-meat stench of its breath.

Hercules was weaponless. He leaped away and ran

toward an oak tree, grasped its trunk near the base, and pulled. Up came the tree, roots and all. The lion was coming too. Hercules raised the uprooted tree like a club and smashed it down on the lion's head. The tree broke to splinters.

The lion struck. Hercules sprang away, but not in time. One claw touched his tunic, ripped it to tatters, and ripped the flesh underneath. Unarmed, naked, bleeding, Hercules ran toward his spear. The lion sniffed at the bloody cloth, then raised its head and calmly watched as Hercules ran uphill. The man knew that as fast as he was running, the beast could catch him any time it wanted. But he kept running, for he couldn't do anything else.

Now the lion was following. The spear grew heavier and heavier as Hercules ran, and he wanted to throw it away, but he didn't; it was his only weapon. The lion was gaining ground at every step. Hercules dodged behind a huge rock and drove his spear deep into the earth behind. Then he planted himself and pulled back on the shaft, trying to lever the enormous boulder out of the ground. The spear bent, but the rock did not budge. And the lion was getting very close. Hercules pulled on the spear; the muscles of back and shoulders writhed like serpents under his bronze flesh. He was breathing red-hot needles; he could hardly see; the rock grew misty. The shaft tried to pull out of his hands as he bent it, but he wouldn't let go. Down, down, he pressed. The spear was bent like a bow now; his hands almost touched the ground. Blackness swarmed in his head; he could do no more. "Zeus help me," he gasped. He made himself draw one more breath, thrusting with his arms,

30

pressing the end of the shaft into the earth, and finally, not quite believing it, felt the rock move.

This tiny movement was joy. The joy became strength. Strength fought with pain, and pain was winning. Now he lay on the spear, flattening it against the earth with his body, using his hands to push the rock. The huge rock leaped out of its hole like a cork out of a bottle and began to roll downhill, flattening bushes, going faster and faster, straight for the lion.

The lion saw it coming. It leaped away but not quite fast enough. The rock hit the beast, bowling it over. Hercules, seeing the lion on the ground, was filled with new energy. He became a blur of motion. He pulled the spear out of the earth and charged downhill. Holding his spear like a vaulting pole and running full speed, he planted the butt of the spear and leaped. The springy wood bent, then sprang up terrifically, flinging him into the air. This time, he didn't let the pole drop. He held on to it and turned it at the top of his leap, then fell holding it point-first.

The lion crouched on its haunches, forepaws raised, ready to rend the falling man with its talons. Hercules struck as he fell. With all his strength, all his joy, and all his fear, he drove the spear down as he fell toward the lion's face. And drove the spike into the only part of the beast not covered by its armorlike hide—the eye. Deep, deep, the spike pierced into the murky brain.

Writhing in agony, the beast flailed with its paws. And Hercules, dodging, felt his back being raked again by the razor claws. But he didn't care, because he could watch the monster, snarling, frothing, dying.

He climbed to his feet and stood over the lion. He

was panting. He had fallen heavily; his whole body felt like one bruise. And now he bled from many wounds. But he felt no pain, just a great singing joy.

His task, however, wasn't quite done. He had been commanded to bring the lion's hide to the king. But the hide was armor; it couldn't be cut by any blade—or, perhaps, only by one. Hercules lifted one of the great paws and studied it. Then he snapped off a claw. It was as big as a hunting knife and sharper than any knife. Using it as a knife, he flayed the lion, rolled the hide into a bloody bundle, hoisted it to his shoulder, and limped downhill toward the river.

He was so tired now that he was dizzy and could hardly make it to the river. But he kept on because he had to cleanse himself before he slept, wash away his own blood and the lion's and treat his wounds with the herbs as Chiron had taught him.

THE HYDRA

ᏀᏀᏀᏀᏀᏀᏀᏀᏀᏀᏀᏀᏀᏀᏀᏀᏀᏀᏀᏀᏀᏀᏀᏀᏀᏀ

THE KING HAD ORDERED THAT RELAYS OF HORSEMEN be posted every twenty miles to the border of Nemea. "Because," he told Copreus, "I want to know without delay how Hercules fares against the lion . . . so if the monster is slain, we can thank the gods for a great victory."

But Copreus knew the king really wanted to hear that Hercules had been killed, not the lion.

And it was Copreus who got the news first. He was in the courtyard when a horseman galloped through the gate. "Good news!" he cried. "Shepherds in Nemea have found vultures feeding on the flesh of a huge carcass. Its hide is gone, and its head, but it must be the lion, for nothing else could be so big."

"Yes," said Copreus. "That's very good news. You deserve a reward for riding here so fast. Why don't you dismount and take the news to the king yourself?"

But he hadn't finished the sentence before the messenger had wheeled his horse about and galloped out the gate again. Copreus was not surprised. Everyone feared the king and tried to keep as far away from him as possible. "I'll have to go tell him myself," he thought. "And I'll be lucky if I come out with my head on my shoulders."

But Copreus was clever. He was the only one who knew how to handle the king at all. He went into the throne room and said, "Oh, king, the people of Nemea are calling you their savior. And they are preparing rich gifts to thank you for sending someone to rid their land of that monster."

"What monster?" cried the king. "The Nemean Lion?"

"Yes, your majesty."

"It's dead?"

"Its flayed body was found on the mountain."

"So it must have been Hercules who killed it."

"No one else, your majesty, but the young man you were wise enough to choose for so dangerous a task."

"He'll be coming back here!" cried the king, shuddering. "He'll insist on seeing me this time. I won't! I won't! I won't see him! Copreus, listen to me carefully. I want a big hole dug right into the courtyard, deep as a well, but wider. And I want paving stones so cut that they will fit over this hole and make a lid, hiding it completely. And I want it furnished like a room, you know, very comfortably, and well provided with food and wine. For, if Hercules ever comes through the gate, I shall enter that pit and stay there until he departs. See to it, man! And if everything is not done exactly as I have described, and very quickly, you shall pay with your head."

35

"I shall do as you wish, your majesty. But would it not be simpler to lock the gate against him as before and station troops outside?"

"Of course I want that done too, you idiot! Try to use your head while it's still on your shoulders. If he can kill that monster and take its hide, what's to stop him from tearing the gate off its hinges and strolling in as he pleases? Do as I say. Dig my pit, furnish it, then go lock the city gate and post troops outside. And be there yourself to meet him when he comes."

"That won't be until the day after tomorrow, at the soonest. It's a two-day trip from Nemea."

"Good. That will give Hera time to think of something else for him to do. I hope she can come up with something really fatal in two days . . ."

The next morning, the king summoned Copreus and said, "Hera appeared to me last night and brought a new task for Hercules. You are to meet him beyond the gate and transmit these instructions."

Copreus listened silently as the king told him of the next labor facing Hercules. As he listened, he felt his bones turning to jelly. "I'm done for," he thought. "When Hercules hears me describe this next monster, he'll squash me like an ant. And if I refuse to take the message, the king will call his ax man, and my head will roll. Either way I'm a goner. The king will kill me today, or Hercules will do it tomorrow. Well, I might as well give myself one more day."

So all he said when the king had finished was, "Yes, your majesty."

But when he returned to his apartment in the castle, he knelt on the floor and wept. For he did not wish to die—either that day or the next.

"Don't cry," said a voice.

He scrambled to his feet. It was his niece, Iole. He hadn't heard her come. She moved very silently, this child, and seemed to appear without approach, like a cat. In fact, she was quite a bit like a cat: slender, graceful, very quick, with black bangs and big green eyes.

"Don't cry," she said. "You'll be all right. I'll tell Hercules about the Hydra."

"How do you know about that?" he shouted.

"I know . . ."

"You've been eavesdropping again!"

"I have to. Nobody tells me anything."

"You silly little hellcat! Do you know what the king would do to you if he caught you hiding in his throne room listening to secret conversations?"

"He never notices anything; he's too busy with himself. Anyway, I'm very hard to see if I don't want to be seen. And that old throne room is full of shadows."

"But what do you mean, *you'll* tell Hercules?"

"Just what I said. I'll do what the king told you to do. I'll meet him outside the walls and tell him he has to kill that dreadful thing."

"I can't let you do that. He'll be very angry when he hears what he has to do."

"I'm not afraid of him."

"You've never seen him."

"Oh, yes I have. I saw him when he first came. I sneaked after you and was hiding behind the gate."

"Well then, you know how big he is."

"Yes . . . and how kindhearted. He won't hurt me. He likes children."

"How can you possibly know that?"

"I know."

HERCULES

When Hercules came to Mycenae, he once again found the city locked against him. Once again, he thought about knocking the gate down and forcing his way into the castle. But then he realized that he really had no wish to see the king, who didn't want to see him. In fact, there was nothing he wanted here but to work off his curse as soon as possible and go back to Thebes or to the centaurs. But he had to wait where he was until someone came to tell him what he had to do next.

He camped outside the city. He stuck his spear in the ground, hung the lion's skin over it, and had a fine tent. He sat in his tent and watched the gate. He expected to see soldiers coming through, then Copreus, bearing a message from the king. No one came through. He waited and waited. He dozed off. When he opened his eyes he saw a girl standing near him.

"Are you awake?" she asked.

"Unless I'm dreaming. Who are you?"

"Iole."

"Hello, Iole."

"Is that the lion skin you're using for a tent?"

"It is."

"I'd like you to tell me all about how you killed it, but I have something to tell you first. Do you remember Copreus?"

"The king's herald? Of course. I expect him to show up soon."

"He won't. I'm here instead."

"I don't understand."

"He's my uncle. But he's afraid to tell you what you have to do, so I will."

"He's afraid to come himself and sent you? What kind of man is he?"

38

"A coward. And the king's worse. But no one sent me exactly. I wanted to come."

"Well, at least you're not afraid of me."

"No sir, I'm not. I have a lot to tell you; shall I start?"

"Please."

"The thing you have to fight next is called the Hydra. I don't exactly know what it is, though. The king's bad at describing things. But it's very big. And very awful. It has a hundred heads—lizard heads or dragon heads—and each head has a hundred teeth, and every tooth is poison. The way I picture it is a hundred crocodiles joined at the waist."

"Where is this charming creature to be found?"

"In Argos, in a grove called Lerna, on the bank of a river. I'm coming with you."

"What?"

"Oh, yes. I watched you when you left to fight the lion, and I wanted to come with you. But we didn't know each other then. Now we do."

"Do you really think I'd let you anywhere near that dragon with a hundred heads?"

"I want to come with you."

"Listen to me, Iona dear . . ."

"Iole."

"Iole dear, I like you very much. I've enjoyed our conversation. And I thank you for bringing me this message, unwelcome though it is. But forget all about me and the Hydra."

She didn't answer. She was gone before he saw her move; she had slipped away like a shadow.

"What a smart brave girl," he said to himself. "I hope I haven't hurt her feelings. But I can't think about that now. I have to prepare for this monster. Yes, this will take a bit of thinking. I wish my brains were as strong as my muscles. Well, I'll do what I can with what I have. Now, what did that child tell me? The Hydra is very poisonous, she said. So even one tooth breaking my skin will kill me. And a hundred mouths times a hundred teeth. Let's see: that's ten thousand deaths coming at me all at once. Hmmmm. Lion skin, you shall be a tent no more; I have a better use for you."

He whisked the lion's hide off the spear that was serving as a tent pole, drew one of the lion's claws from his pouch, and, using it as a knife, cut the skin into a long-sleeved tunic and a pair of trousers reaching down to his ankles. He also made gauntlets and boots—for he wanted not one inch of himself exposed to the Hydra's poison teeth. "If this hide turned aside my spear and my arrows," he thought, "it should blunt the Hydra's bite. I need a helmet, too." He took the lion's head and made a helmet of it. It covered his face when he put it on; he could breathe through the mouth and look out the eyeholes.

"It's very hot in here," said Hercules to himself. "The Hydra may not have to kill me; I may just roast to death before I get to him."

All this time, Iole had been watching him from behind a tree. For she hadn't the slightest notion of going home. She had decided to go wherever Hercules went, and if he wouldn't take her, she would simply follow him without letting him see her. She was very good at that.

She watched as Hercules took off his lion-skin clothing, wrapped it into a bundle, and slung it on his back. He grasped his spear and set off for the grove at Lerna where the Hydra dwelt. He traveled for three days and never noticed the girl gliding from shadow of tree to shelter of bush as she followed him.

The grove called Lerna is tucked inside an elbow of the river. In this river lurked the monstrous reptile. Every day it crawled out to kill. The trees of the grove grow right down to the river, but stop short at one spot; there grass grows from wood to water. Here in this meadow Hercules waited for the Hydra to crawl out of the river.

It was a summer morning, and the sun was hot. Hercules wore his long-sleeved tunic, and trousers, and boots, and gauntlets, and helmet. He felt himself roasting alive in the heavy lion pelt. "If that Hydra doesn't come soon," he thought, "he'll find a cooked meal all laid out for him."

And, as Hercules waited near the river, Iole waited in the grove. She was crouched behind a tree, so well hidden that he couldn't have seen her even if he had turned suddenly. But she had a clear view.

The last monster Hercules had fought was the Nemean Lion, which had roared terribly as it came. And he was expecting the Hydra to announce itself thunderously out of its hundred mouths. So he was taken by surprise when the Hydra came out of the river silently, like a reptile, and had almost reached Hercules before he saw what was coming.

He couldn't believe what he saw. It was a crocodile, but the size of ten crocodiles. "This can't be it," he thought. "It has just one head. But what else can it be? That river can't hold two monsters."

But he was very glad that there was only one head to cope with, even if that one head was as big as a dragon's, full of sharp teeth. He dropped his bow and

spear and drew his sword. The Hydra slithered toward him. Weighed down as he was by the heavy lion pelt, Hercules nonetheless leaped into the air and landed on the Hydra's back. He raised his sword high in both hands, slashed down in a terrific scything blow, saw his blade cut through the knobby hide, and felt it slice through flesh and giant bone—right through the entire neck. The Hydra's head seemed to leap off its body. Blood poured out of the neck stump, black blood, smoking as it fell, charring the grass, turning the greenness to black dust.

And Hercules was amazed to see the cut-off head sliding toward him. It sprang off the ground, snapping at him. He struck it down with his clenched fist, whirled about, and saw something that almost made him drop his sword and run. The stump of neck had split into two stumps; from each neck sprouted a new head.

He struck again, cutting off both heads with one blow. They fell to the grass, blood hissing. They did not die, but snapped about his legs like mad dogs. They couldn't bite through his lion-hide trousers, but held on, trying to drag him down. And now, instead of two neck stumps, there were four, and each stump grew a new head. The four heads struck at him with sickening force. Four pairs of jaws clamped onto his body. The teeth couldn't pierce the pelt, but they closed with crushing power. He felt his bones must break. Jaws held his arms; he couldn't raise his sword. He tore himself away and tried to run clear, but the cut-off heads were fastened to his legs. They dragged him down.

He forced himself up. His sword whirled in a blur about his head. One after the other, he cut the four heads off. Now these heads fell and joined the pack of heads ravening about. Where the four heads had been, there were now eight heads. They came at him from everywhere now, clamping him from all directions. His arms and legs were locked by jaws. Three pair of jaws held his waist, jaws were locking on his head, blinding him. Inside the lion-hide helmet, he felt his skull being squeezed to a pulp. Calling on his last strength, he whirled and kicked and chopped and stabbed. He tore himself free and tried to run. But all the heads were fastened on his legs now; they pulled him down as a pack of hounds pulls down a deer.

Lying on the ground, he saw a pair of jaws striking down toward his face. Before he could stop himself, he slashed with his sword, slicing off that head—and knew it was the worst thing he could have done. For now two heads would grow, and he knew he couldn't handle any more.

The pain was too much now; he felt himself going. And just then he saw Iole flash past him, carrying a torch.

"Stop!" he shouted.

But she ran straight toward the Hydra and slashed at it with her fiery torch, searing the neck stump, then seemed to melt into air, she moved so quickly, dodging away. Hercules smelled the stench of burning flesh. The Hydra flopped gigantically; it was in agony. Its mouths were shrieking. Through his fog, Hercules saw that the burned flesh of the stump was not sprouting any new head.

He saw Iole scoop up the torch and run toward him. She whirled the torch, beating back the pack of cut-off heads. She whipped them with flame, beating them away from his legs. Hercules staggered to his feet.

44

"Cut off the heads!" cried Iole. "I'll burn the stumps!"

But Iole was clad only in a thin tunic. Hercules realized that one scratch of a poison tooth would kill her on the spot. He snatched the torch from her, with his left hand seized her by the waist, swung her off the ground, and hurled her into the river. Then he picked up his sword and crouched, waiting for the Hydra to come at him again.

In one hand he held the torch, in his other hand, the sword. And strength had returned. The thought of the child risking her life that way drove out all fear, all weakness. The fire of the torch seemed to be burning cleanly in his veins.

The Hydra was upon him. He moved swiftly, dodging, striking, twisting away from the jaws, slashing again. Each sword blow cut off a head. And, as soon as he struck with his sword, he struck with his torch, searing the neck stump, burning the flesh so that no new head could grow.

He was very weary now. He could hardly move. But the monster still had two heads left. Hercules did not wait for the Hydra to attack. Forcing his legs to move, he charged. He whirled his sword, cutting off the last two heads, then struck with his torch, searing the last two stumps.

Now the Hydra was blind. The great leather body was twitching. The spiked tail was flailing. The neck stalks were wriggling like charred worms, but life was going out of the monster. The tail flopped weakly, like a grounded fish. The neck stalks went limp. Then all movement stopped. And when the body died, the heads on the grass died also.

Hercules lifted the heavy helmet from his head, drinking the air. He cast off the tunic and slid out of the heavy trousers. No tooth had pierced his armor; he was unscratched. But the air was scorched and he felt poisoned all the same. He didn't take his gauntlets off, or his boots. He had one more thing to do before he could bathe in the river. He emptied his quiver of arrows and, one by one, dipped them in the hissing pools of Hydra blood.

"I'll need special weapons," he thought, "if each monster I fight is worse than the last one. Now these arrows will kill whatever they touch."

He dipped the last arrow, then kicked his way through the dead grinning heads as he tramped toward the river.

When he dived in, Iole climbed out. She stood on the bank and watched him swim. The sun was low now, painting the river with fire. It was still warm, and Iole's tunic was almost dry when Hercules climbed out of the river. He didn't say anything. He sat on a rock and beckoned to her. She came toward him slowly and stopped a few feet away.

He spoke softly. "You saved my life, you know."

"And got thrown into the river for it. My, you threw me far. It was like flying."

"You're a very brave girl. And a very clever one. And very, very naughty. You're going straight back home."

She smiled and came closer, looking up at him with big green eyes. Before he knew what she was doing, she had leaped onto his lap as lightly as a kitten. "But I live with you now," she purred. "I've decided to marry you when I'm older."

46

"You'd better pick someone else. I don't think I'll last that long."

"I don't want anyone else. And you have to last. I'm going wherever you go. You just saw how useful I can be."

"You're going back home. You live with your uncle, don't you? In the castle?"

"With my Uncle Copreus and that mean old king. Do you really want me to live in a place like that? If you take me back there, I'll run away again. And if I can't find you, I'll live in the woods and get eaten by bears."

"How would you like to live in a cheerful castle with beautiful kind people?"

"With you?"

"With my parents, in Thebes."

"I want to be with you."

"Well, I'll visit you between times."

"Do you promise?"

"I do."

"And will you marry me when I grow up."

"If you still want me then, I'll be honored."

And they went off together. But had they stayed a bit longer, they would have seen a wonderful thing. The cut-off Hydra heads sank out of sight, and where each had been, a spring bubbled up. The waters of these springs flowed together and became a river, which swallowed the river Lerna and became a deep swift-running river of crystal waters so pure and beautiful that it gave the name "hydra" to water forever.

THE AUGEAN STABLES

THE WORLD'S WORST CATTLE THIEF LIVED IN A PLACE called Elis. The people there hated him, not only because he stole their cattle, but because of what he did with them afterward. Being a thief himself, he thought everybody else was too, and was always afraid someone would steal the cattle he had stolen. So he built a huge barn and holding pen big enough for a thousand cows and fifty bulls, and he never let them out, nor did he ever bother about cleaning the place. Of course, it grew filthier and filthier. Mountains of muck grew. People called it the biggest dung heap in the world. His neighbors sold their farms and moved to the other side of the wide river because the place stank. And he just laughed. His neighbors were so eager to sell that they took any price offered and soon he owned all the land around.

He was a huge fat man. His face was always greasy, and his hair crawled with lice. His name was Augeas.

When he bought up the last farm in the country, he called himself "Lord of the Manor." Others called him "Lord of the Manure," but not where he could hear them.

To clean out these filthy stables was Hercules' next labor.

He learned about it when he came back to Mycenae after killing the Hydra. He didn't come back immediately. He had gone to Thebes first to leave Iole with his parents. He very much wanted to stay there himself and had to tear himself away. And on the road back, he had a great longing to visit Thessaly and his old tutor, Chiron, and to run with the centaurs in the hills. But Hera's curse weighed heavily on him, and he knew he had to get back to his labors.

Again the gate was locked. Again he waited outside the walls. Again Copreus came through the gate, but this time he came alone.

"Hail, friend," called Hercules. "Where's the army?"

"I left them home," said Copreus.

"Do you bear a message from the king?"

"I do."

"Another labor?"

"Yes."

"How do you dare to come alone? Last time you were afraid to come at all. You sent your niece."

"Yes," said Copreus, "and I have learned from the child. She said you were kind. I didn't believe her then, but I do now. I hear you've adopted her."

"Not exactly. I think she's adopted me. She's with my parents in Thebes and will live with them. She doesn't like it here."

"No, this is no place for her. I thank you for taking her to Thebes, and I regret very much what I am about to tell you."

"Tell it, man, tell it. Whatever it is, I know you are not to blame."

"Well, I'm going to live up to my name of the dung man now, because I'm going to tell you about the biggest pile of dung in the world."

And Copreus told Hercules about the fat cattle thief and his filthy stables.

"If I understand you," said Hercules, "this Augeas has penned a thousand cattle for a thousand days, and has never let them out. So the place is a filthy reeking midden, and you can smell it all the way to Egypt. Very well, I understand all that. What about it?"

"You are to go there and clean it up in one day."

"That is my next task?"

"Yes. It should make a change. You won't have to fight anything big and dreadful, or kill any monsters who are trying to kill you. Just a day's cleaning, that's all."

"Copreus, I know none of this is your fault; you're only the king's messenger, and I'm very fond of your niece who saved my life. But you'd better get out of here before I lose my temper."

Hercules watched him scurry away. "An easy one, this time," he said to himself. "No monsters to fight, no claws or spiked tails or poison fangs coming at me . . . just a day's work, mucking out stables used by a thousand animals for a thousand days. By the gods, I'd rather take on the lion and the Hydra in one afternoon. My strength and speed won't help me this time, nor my spear that can split an oak tree, nor my deadly arrows. This requires thinking. And I don't have the beginnings of an idea. Oh well, I'll be a week walking to Elis; perhaps something will occur to me on the way, though I doubt it."

Scowling and muttering to himself, he turned his back on the city and began once again a journey he didn't want to take.

When Hercules reached the river Alpheus, he knew that he had only a few more miles to go. He stopped to look at the broad rippling river, wishing he could just wander along the shore and forget all about the filthy task awaiting him.

"Well," he thought, "the sooner I start, the sooner I'll finish." He began to walk on, but stopped because he heard a little snuffling sound. There, hiding behind a tree, was a maiden in a blue dress, hands over her face, sobbing.

Hercules went to her and said, "Why are you crying?"

"I'm to be the bride of the river, and I'm afraid . . . afraid . . ."

"What do you mean, 'bride of the river'?"

"Of the River-god—that's what he calls himself. River-demon is more like it. Many rivers run through my country, which is Calydon. I am Dienera, princess of Calydon. And the River-god told my father, the king, he'd flood the whole country, sweeping away farms and villages and cities, unless he could have me as his wife. And to save his kingdom, my father brought me here."

Her violet eyes filled with tears. They overflowed and rolled down her cheeks.

51

"Don't cry," said Hercules.

"I'm so frightened."

"Well, I don't see any reason for you to marry anyone you don't want to," said Hercules.

A mist arose from the river. It became a column of mist and thickened into the shape of a giant turtle standing upright. It spoke in a low grating voice.

"Leave this place or you die."

"Who are you?" said Hercules.

"I am the River-god."

"Is this where you live, here in the river Alpheus?"

"I dwell in all the inland waters, as I choose. Right now I am here, and I wish you elsewhere."

"Why?"

"That girl is meant to be my wife."

"Who means her to be?"

"I do."

"How about you?" said Hercules to the girl. "Do you want him for a husband?"

She shook her head silently. Hercules saw that she was afraid to speak.

"The princess doesn't like the idea," said Hercules. "Swim away now like a good fellow."

He felt something touch him and looked down. Dienera had put her hand on his arm. She reached up and pulled his head down so that she could whisper into his ear. "Take care. He's very evil. He changes form at will. If he doesn't snap your head off as that giant turtle, he'll turn into a dreadful horned fish. If he doesn't kill you that way, he'll dive into the river and make it flood until it drowns you. If you try to flee, he'll overflow his banks and chase you through meadows and fields, sweeping everything away in his flood, until he catches you and drowns you."

"Thank you for the warning," said Hercules, "but I'll have to fight him if I'm to save you. I can't do it today, though. I have another job to do first. I'll be back tomorrow. Will you be safe until then?"

"I don't know. I'm so frightened."

"Tell him you'll be his bride. But you need two days to make your wedding gown."

"But then in two days I'll have to marry him."

"I promise to be back tomorrow and fight him for you. I can't promise to win, but I'll try. Farewell."

He raced away, knowing that if she looked at him again out of her brimming eyes, he'd forget all about his task and stay where he was. As he hurried on, he began to smell something. It was a beautiful summer day, and among the meadow grass was flowering clover, one of the sweetest scents in the world, but he wasn't smelling clover now. It was something foul. It grew worse and worse.

"That must be the stables," he thought. "If I can't stand the smell at this distance, what will I do when I get there?"

He thought a moment, then ran back a way and searched among the grass. "Well for me now that Chiron taught me herbs," he thought. He plucked great handfuls of what he had found, which was wild garlic. Then he unslung his lion-skin helmet, packed it full of the wild garlic, and stuck it on his head. It was hard to breathe. And what he was breathing was the fumes of wild garlic, but they blocked the foul stench coming from the farm.

In the distance, he saw an enormous barn, so big it covered ten acres. The barnyard was guarded by a high fence. Through the fence, he saw shapes moving. Before he reached the gate, he heard a racketing yell:

"Stop!"

He stopped. Facing him was a grossly fat man, gnawing on a raw beef bone and spitting out bits of gristle. "Who are you, lion-face?" asked the man.

"My name is Hercules. Who are you?"

"I am Augeas. I own this barn and all these cattle. And I own you too now, for a day, because your master has sent you to me to muck out my stables. Right? That's why you're here, isn't it?"

"That's right," said Hercules.

"Well, get a shovel and start working. But you'd better take off that lion mask first; you'll scare my cattle."

Now, the helmet had slipped a bit, and Hercules couldn't quite see out the eyeholes. He adjusted the helmet and looked at the man again—and gasped in amazement. For the fat face had huge ballooning cheeks and seven chins, but no nose at all.

"May I ask you two questions, sir?" said Hercules.

"Make 'em short."

"Why do you keep your place so filthy?"

The man hopped up and down in glee, waving his beef bone and laughing a phlegmy laugh. "Harr, harr, harr. Stink 'em out, Here! Stink 'em out and grab off their farms, pile up the acres, and get rich! Next question."

"Were you born without a nose, or did someone cut it off?"

"Neither one. Cut it off myself."

"Why?"

"That makes three questions. But all right. I cut it off so I couldn't smell what I was doing. Very useful, having no nose. You can do all sorts of dirty profitable things. That's what I tell any ambitious young person, 'Cut off your nose!' Told it to my own son, but he wouldn't listen, the little fool—just ran away."

As he spoke, he led Hercules through the gate into the barnyard. The man kept talking, but Hercules wasn't listening; he was busy looking. And what he saw sickened him. Piles of manure towered higher than the barn roof. The animals packed into the yard were so crusted with filth you couldn't tell whether they were cows or bulls. And the flies! Great swarms of fat blue-bottle flies covering every surface, clustering so thickly you couldn't pick out a single fly, just one huge hideous glinting blue gob.

"I'll never be able to clean this place," said Hercules to himself. "Not in a year, let alone one day. But if I fail in even one task, I can't work off my curse, and the vision that Hera sent me will come true. Never! I won't let that happen, no matter what. I'll go back right now and fight the River-god and get myself drowned—and cheat my fate that way."

He pushed Augeas aside, rushed out the gate, and raced away over the field. He heard the man shouting after him, but paid him no heed. He ran as hard as he could because he wanted to get away from the stench as soon as possible; he could feel it now coming through the packing of wild garlic. But as he ran, he found himself thinking about how he would fight the River-god.

"What did she say he changes into? First a giant snapping turtle, then a horned fish, and if his enemy is still alive, he makes the river flood up, drowning every-thing. Hmmmm. That gives me the beginning of an idea. Yes . . . just the beginning, though. Well, I think better when I'm fighting. Maybe before I finish tussling with that watery demon, I'll have a whole idea."

He found Dienera hiding behind the same tree. "You're back early," she whispered.

"Listen, princess," he said. "I've never kissed any woman except my mother, but I want to kiss you now. Nothing serious—just to make the River-god jealous."

"Is that the only reason you want to kiss me?"

"It's to make him come out of the river, you see. So I can get at him."

She sighed. He bent down and kissed her cheek.

When the River-god had appeared before, he had risen as a column of mist which had thickened into the shape of a giant snapping turtle. Hercules expected him to do the same thing now but was amazed to see a huge plate spinning out of the water. It landed near him, and he saw that it was the turtle, looking like a double disk of armor plate because it had pulled in arms and legs to leap out of the river. It stuck out a leathery lizard head and scuttled toward him on leather legs. Turtles are supposed to be slow; this one was fast as a tiger. It rushed toward him and snapped at his leg, which he just managed to pull away in time. He danced around, dodging its furious rushes. The great jaws were snap-ping with enough force to bite through flesh and muscle and thick bone, to shear his leg off at the hip.

The turtle had moved so swiftly that Hercules had no time to draw a weapon, nor to don his lion-skin armor. He ran into the forest hoping the turtle would have trouble following him, but it slithered swiftly over the fallen brush and was after him in a flash. Without breaking stride, he grasped a young oak and pulled it out of the ground with a mighty yank. Whirling, he lifted the uprooted tree as high as he could and smashed it down at the turtle. The tree struck square, shattering the shell. The naked turtle turned and scuttled toward the river. Hercules raced after, hoping to catch it and finish it off before it could enter the water. The turtle was too fast; it slid into the river and disappeared.

And immediately reappeared—not as a turtle, but as a huge fish, twenty feet long, whose head narrowed into a long sharp bony prong. This was the River-god's second change: the horned fish.

The fish was more terrible than the turtle. It flung itself out of the water and came flying through the air, aiming its horn straight at Hercules' throat. He swung his arm, batting it aside, but the horn ripped a bloody furrow in his arm. He ran; the fish followed, slithering on its belly like a snake . . . swiftly . . . swiftly. Hercules ran as fast as he could to where his things lay scattered. He stooped as he ran, scooping up a lion-hide gauntlet, and whirled just as the fish leaped at him again. But this time he grasped the fish's horn with the hand that wore the gauntlet made of the hide that nothing could pierce. He held the threshing fish at arm's length by its knife-edge horn and whipped it up and down, faster and faster, finally snapping his wrist and breaking the horn off clean. He stabbed the fish with its own horn. It flopped to the water, leaving a trail of blood.

He heard Dienera's voice: "Run, Hercules, run! He'll flood his banks and drown you!"

"Aha, that's it," shouted Hercules. "Now I know what I was trying to think of. He fights first as a turtle, then as a fish, and now he will flood his banks trying to drown me. He will pursue me over the fields, washing everything away as he goes. Well, chase away, flood! Catch me if you can!"

Laughing, shouting, Hercules swept up Dienera in his arms and fled the river bank just as the water boiled up in a mighty crest, gushed over its banks, and hurled itself over the fields, breaking down trees as it went, sweeping up fallen logs, and tossing them about like twigs, raging across the country in a foaming avalanche of water.

He raced ahead of the flood, heading straight back the way he had come, toward the stables of Augeas. The brown frothing water, laced with trees, was almost at his heels. But he kept ahead of it, running very swiftly although he bore Dienera in his arms. Now he saw the barn roof looming in the middle distance, and the piles of dung, and the clotted shape of the cattle.

He saw Augeas running to meet him shaking his fist and yelling something he couldn't hear. Then the fat man saw the wall of water, turned again, and ran for the barnyard. But too slowly; he was too fat to run fast. Hercules flashed past him and heard a gurgling scream but did not stop to look back.

He ran through the gates, the river tumbling after. He ran straight through, circling the barn, and around to the other side of the fence, not daring to turn lest he should lose a stride, but hearing the roar of the water behind him. He leaped the fence on the other side and kept running.

Now the noise changed, lost its roar, became a gulping sucking sound, fell to a scraping, then to a wet whisper. He stopped, panting, and put Dienera down. He turned and looked back. The river, sweeping through the Augean stables, had choked itself on the mountains of dung, had silted itself almost solid, and was now crawling back toward its own banks.

Back, back, the river shrank, Hercules and Dienera following it slowly. And he marveled at what the waters had done. Where the barn had been, with its towers of manure and its seething carpet of flies, all was clean, muddy but clean. The stench was gone; the air smelled fresh and wet. Cows and bulls milled about, drenched and shiny, mooing in confusion because they had forgotten what they looked like. The barn was down; it was a wreckage of clean boards.

Hercules looked at Dienera. She smiled up at him; it was the first time he had seen her smile.

"I don't think the river will bother you again," he said. "It'll be busy for a while, digesting its last meal."

"Yes, thank you."

"What now? Back to Calydon?"

"Where are you going?"

"Back to Mycenae to find out what I have to do next. Something dreadful, no doubt, but it can't be worse than this job. You were a great help to me, you know, you and your watery wooer. It took a flood to clean this mess."

"I didn't do anything—just stood around being frightened. You're very brave and very strong."

"Shall I take you back to Calydon?"

"Am I really the first girl you ever kissed?"

"Except my mother."

"Do you think you'd like to again sometime?"

"It's possible. But I won't have much time for kissing and such until I finish my labors."

"Will you visit me in Calydon between adventures?"

"I'll try."

"No, that means you won't, and I want you to. Don't you want to?"

"Yes, but—"

He saw her eyes brimming with tears again.

"Please don't cry."

"How can I help it when you're making me sad?"

"All right, I promise to come see you in Calydon."

"When?"

"Soon."

She blinked away her tears and smiled at him so sweetly that he bent down again and kissed her wet face.

THE BLIND MAN

THERE WAS AN OLD BLIND MAN WHO HAD NO HOME OF his own but wandered from place to place and was welcome, at first, wherever he went because he knew what was going to happen before it happened. That kind of person is called an oracle. There were many of them then, but the blind man was the best.

He had never wanted to be an oracle. He didn't like to look into the future, but he couldn't help it.

Now, as it happened, this Blind Man came to Thebes and was wandering about the market place when Iole saw him. She marveled at the way he made his way through the crowd without bumping into anyone. She knew he was blind; she had darted up to look into his face and had seen that his large eyes had pupil and iris all one color, a milky blue, staring stonily straight ahead. He used a cane, not tap-tapping, but holding it in front of him like a pointer. He was shopping. He

63

stopped at an oven and bought a loaf of barley bread, stopped at a woman sitting among baskets and bought a bunch of new onions and a wedge of cheese. He asked for things in a deep rolling voice and made the women take money for what he had bought. And Iole, seeing these women trying to refuse his coins and knowing how they would fight each other in the street for a penny, thought that the Blind Man must be some kind of wizard. She decided to follow him.

She followed him through the market, followed him as he made his way through the teeming square into the quieter avenue. She flitted silently after him through the city, through the gates, beyond the walls, and kept with him as he headed toward the open country. He filled his flask at a stream, sat on a rock, and began to eat his bread and cheese and onions. Iole stood silently, watching him.

"Want something to eat?" he called.

Iole didn't answer.

"You there, girl, are you hungry?"

"How do you know I'm here?" said Iole.

"You've been following me since I came to the market."

"You're not blind at all; you're just pretending."

"Why would anyone pretend that?"

"Can you see me or not?"

"No."

"Then how do you know I'm a girl? Well, you know now because you've heard my voice. But before?"

"I know more than that. I know how old you are. I know that you look like an Egyptian temple cat with black bangs and jade eyes."

"How? How?"

"Everyone is surrounded by a band of colored light—red, green, blue, purple, all the colors, and every band is different. I feel the colors on my face; they prickle in different ways. Also, my nose is as sharp as a hunting dog's, and my ears are as keen as a bat's. The goddess who took my sight sharpened my other senses and gave me some extra ones."

"Which goddess?"

"The Owl Goddess, Pallas Athena, stern and wise."

"Why did she take your sight? Why was she so cruel?"

"She wanted me to serve her. She wanted me not to be misled by appearances but to pay perfect attention to signs and clues by which the gods make their meaning known."

"Will you be my grandfather?"

"What?"

"Be my grandfather."

"I've never had wife or child, certainly no grandchildren."

"But I'm adopting you as my grandfather. Now you must adopt me as your granddaughter, so it'll come out even."

"Do you always go around adopting people?"

"You're only the second. Hercules was the first."

"Hercules!"

"I met him at Mycenae, where I used to live. I helped to kill the Hydra. Then I adopted him as my husband for when I grow up. That's why I'm here. He brought me here to live with his mother and father in the castle. What colors am I?"

"Different shades of green. April green like new grass. Cat's-eye green. Black green of the sharp spring shadows. And a greenish silvery brown of the new moon."

"What do I smell like?"

"April leaves. Pebbles picked from the bottom of a stream. New grass."

"You must stay here and tell me things, and not go away."

"But that's what I do: go away. I tell things and go away . . . because people don't like what I say."

"I'll like whatever you say. I promise."

"You don't understand. The goddess blinded me so I could see what is to be. It's a cruel, cruel gift."

"Why?"

"People ask me to tell their fortunes. And I say no, because what I see, usually, is misfortune. But they beg. And I tell them. And when it comes true, they blame me, as if I had *made* it happen."

"Suppose it's something good?"

"Then they think they did it all themselves."

"Well, I'll go where you go. It'll be a few years before I can marry Hercules, and I'll come back here then."

"Do you mean it about marrying Hercules?"

"Oh, yes."

"Do you love him?"

"Oh, yes."

"You mustn't."

"Why not?"

"Poor child, poor dear child. My blind eyes pierce the darkness of time to come, and I wish they did not. What I see is this: Hercules cannot be killed by living man or god or monster. Painted in fire upon the blackness be-

fore my eyes is she who will be his doom, a girl who wants to marry him."

"Oh, no!"

She began to sob.

"Come here, child."

She ran into his arms. He stroked her head. "Don't cry."

"I love him so. I don't want anyone to kill him. Why do you say such terrible things?"

"Forgive me. I don't mean to."

"Anyway, how do you know? I don't believe there is such a thing as the future. If you believe that, you think nothing can ever change. Don't you see?"

"I am blind."

"Oh, you know what I mean."

"Perhaps you mean more than I know. Perhaps you can teach me what the goddess didn't. All the same, I think you'd better be careful about loving Hercules. For my vision of his fate is terrible, and I can tell you only what it is given me to see."

"Let's leave this place, Grandfather."

"Does it matter where we go?"

"No."

"Come then . . ."

THE TRIPLE TERROR

⅁⅁⅁⅁⅁⅁⅁⅁⅁⅁⅁⅁⅁⅁⅁⅁⅁⅁⅁⅁⅁⅁⅁⅁⅁⅁⅁⅁⅁

HERCULES' NEXT TASK CONCERNED A CATTLE BREEDER also, but quite unlike the filthy Augeas. For the herd of bulls belonging to Geryon was the finest in all the world. Blood-red they were, huge and sleek, with coral nostrils and jet-black horns.

Geryon himself was a truly monstrous figure, what might be called a Siamese triplet: three giant bodies joined at the waist. Complete bodies. Three heads, six arms, six legs. In a fight he was complete havoc. He had been known to take on a whole company of warriors single-handed and kill every one. With his six legs he could outrun the fastest horse. For sport, he wrestled three bears at once and always won.

And now, Hercules had been ordered to go to Geryon's island and steal his herd of bulls. Hercules stood listening as Copreus told him of this new task. As usual, they stood outside the city walls, because the king

69

was still afraid to let Hercules anywhere near him.

"Well," said Hercules. "I haven't used my poison arrows against anyone yet, but I may have to start now. This three-bodied monster sounds dangerous."

"I should tell you something else," said Copreus. "There is a prophecy concerning Geryon—that he can be killed by no one else—so you may have to steal his cattle without fighting him."

"Is that possible?"

"I don't think so. He has three enormous bulldogs watching them by day. And at night, he watches them himself. And since he has three heads, one of them always stays awake. Others have tried to steal those handsome red bulls and have been torn to pieces by Geryon before they went three paces into the pasture."

"Sounds worse and worse," said Hercules. "But I've done things before that no one thought I could do. Maybe I'll get lucky again."

He turned, and once again began a journey to where he didn't want to go.

Geryon's island lay about ten miles offshore. Hercules stood at the edge of the beach and squinted, trying to make it out in the distance. He saw something, but couldn't tell whether it was an island or a cloud bank. He walked into the surf, then let the tide take him out. He dived, swam underwater, kicked to the surface, then floated, taking great breaths of salt air. Then he began to stroke toward the island. Ten miles was just a refreshing swim for Hercules, and swimming was the best way to get to the island without anyone seeing him.

It was dark when he reached the island. For all his size, Hercules could move through the woods without making a sound. He had learned this from the centaurs.

Nevertheless, when he reached a clearing in the forest which was the bulls' pasture, he heard a terrific racket of howling and barking. Three enormous bulldogs were racing about, circling the herd, ready to mangle anyone who came into the pasture. He faded back into the woods, searched for a hollow tree, took out a honeycomb, then searched for a blackberry bush. He ate honey and blackberries, drank water from a stream, and lay down to sleep.

In the morning, he went silently through the woods until he came to the edge of a field where stood a large stone tower which was Geryon's home. He stayed there all day, watching Geryon as he came and went, studying his habits. The monster dined outdoors. His table was a massive slab of wood laid upon four tree stumps. Hercules had never seen a creature eat the way Geryon did. Every two hours, three cooks laid out three meals on the great table, for each of the bodies favored a different food. The right-hand body liked pork, the middle body liked mutton, and the left-hand body ate barbecued goat meat.

"None of him eats beef," thought Hercules. "I suppose that's because of those beautiful bulls; he likes to think of them as alive, not as meat."

Every two hours on the dot the three meals came out on loaded trays, and the three-bodied monster devoured his pork, his mutton, and his barbecued goat. And when he left the tower and went down to the pasture to visit his herds, if two hours had passed, then the cooks would bring his meals down to the pasture and set them out on the grass, which made the bulldogs happy, because he tossed them the marrow bones.

That afternoon, Hercules had a chance to see Geryon

71

in action. As the monster shambled through the forest, he was attacked by a panther which leaped from a tree straight at his throat. It was like a kitten attacking a bear. Geryon's huge powerful hands grasped each of the panther's paws, holding them in a grip of iron, allowing it no chance to use its claws. And the third pair of hands fastened upon the great cat's neck and strangled it to death.

"Impressive," said Hercules to himself, "but I've handled beasts even bigger. Let me really test that prophecy."

Geryon was sprawled at his table taking an afternoon nap. He did not bother to keep one head awake because he was not watching his herd. Now all six eyes were closed, and the monster was snoring hoarsely. Hercules notched an arrow and drew the bowstring back, back, bending the bow almost double, in the long-armed pull that could send the shaft through a stone wall three feet thick. The arrow whistled through the air. Hercules was amazed to see the air thicken around the flying arrow. The bright air jelled, became murky, a quivering semi-solid mass, like a beached jellyfish. The arrow slowed, stopped, and was held one inch from the sleeping Geryon's head. Then the air cleared as suddenly as it had thickened. The jellied murk faded into sunlight. The arrow fell to the ground. And not one of Geryon's eyes opened.

"Truly," thought Hercules, "the prophecy was right. Some god or demon is shielding him from harm. He cannot be overcome by force. And yet, vanquish him I must, for I shall not be able to take his herd while he is alive."

Hercules went back into the depths of the wood. He had a lot of thinking to do. He thought and thought.

"Prophecies always have a trick in them somewhere," he said to himself. "Chiron taught me that. What does it say? 'Geryon can be killed by no one else.' No one else . . . What does *else* mean? It means another creature. He cannot be killed by any other creature, then. But there are three of him. Perhaps there's an idea there. Yes, I'll test my idea. And if it doesn't work, then I'll have put myself into Geryon's power, into the reach of those six awful hands. But I've got to take the risk."

Hercules went hunting. He was disappointed in not being able to fight Geryon, and he needed violent action. He chased a wild goat, chased it up into the highest crags, leaping from rock to rock, finally seizing it in mid-leap and bearing it, kicking and butting, halfway down the mountain, where he tied it by the horns to a pine tree. Then he went down off the mountain, into the woods, and hunted a wild boar. At that time, of all the animals that hunters pursued, the wild boar was the most savage. It was built low; it was very heavy and very fast, with razor-sharp tusks. Hercules used no weapon. All he donned were his lion-skin gauntlets that no blade could cut. He chased the boar until it turned, for a boar will run until it is cornered, then it will charge.

He cornered the boar between a rock and a fallen tree, stood off a bit, and waited. The boar charged. Hercules knelt, and as the giant pig came toward him, slashing with its razor tusks, he shot out his hands, covered by the gauntlets. He caught a tusk in each hand, stood up, lifting the boar clear off the ground, then

73

slammed it to earth again, knocking its wind out. He slung the boar over his shoulder and carried it back halfway up the mountain to where he had tied the wild goat. Now he bound the boar to another tree, using a chain this time, because a boar can use its tusks to slash through the strongest rope.

The sheep was easy. Sheep are tame. But they are also heavy. And it was hard work carrying the woolly animal up the mountain road on his third trip. But he did, and tied the sheep to another tree.

Now the goat was tethered to one tree, the boar to another, the sheep to a third.

"That's the easy part," said Hercules to himself. "The rest is going to be tricky."

It was noon now and very hot, and he needed a rest. Besides, he knew that Geryon ate at noon, and he wanted to do what he had to do just before it was time for the monster's next meal. So he took a brief nap. Then he woke up and went down to the pasture where the red bulls were cropping grass. Without hesitation, he stepped out from behind a tree into the open space. The three bulldogs bowled down at him. He ran to meet them and slapped them to the ground. They couldn't bite through the lion-hide gauntlets, but his legs were bleeding by the time he had tied their tails together. But tie them together he did. They ran howling in circles, trying to pull themselves apart. He strolled off, lifted a bull to his shoulders, and trotted out of the pasture.

He trotted all the way to Geryon's tower and came walking to the great table, bearing the bull on his shoulders, just as the three cooks were coming out of the tower with their heaping trays of roast pork, roast mutton, and barbecued goat. Geryon saw a stranger coming toward him bearing one of his precious bulls. With a triple bellow, he leaped up and barged through the line of cooks, upsetting the trays of food, and charged toward Hercules, who immediately turned and fled.

Now, it has been told that Geryon was as speedy as he was powerful, that running on six legs he could outrace the fastest horse. And it was true. Nevertheless, Hercules kept ahead of him. The young man had reached his full size now; he was eight feet tall. His legs were as long as a deer's but cabled with muscle. Even carrying a bull on his shoulders, he kept easily ahead of the scuttling Geryon, keeping always the same distance ahead, never running out of sight because he wanted the monster to keep following him. Sometimes he would lag a little, so that Geryon would think he was tiring and would keep chasing him.

Indeed, there was no chance that Geryon would stop chasing him. The three-bodied giant was running in a red mist of rage, and his rage was growing and growing, not only because his bull was being stolen, but because he had been running for two hours now. He had missed one meal and was about to miss a second, and hunger was clawing his belly.

Hercules ran him around the island twice more, then decided he'd better start his final lap. For he himself was getting tired. He was sweating. The bull was growing heavier and heavier; it was struggling and was getting very hard to hold. He tried to put on more speed, but he didn't have enough left; the bull was too heavy. He looked behind and saw that Geryon was gaining on

75

him. He almost stumbled, but caught himself. He knew that if he once fell within reach of those terrible hands it would be the end of him.

There was only one thing to do. He lifted the bull and let it fall, doing it carefully so that the animal landed on its legs and was able to gallop off. He knew that Geryon was so enraged that he would keep chasing him anyway. And he was right. Geryon ignored the bull and plowed on after Hercules, who, relieved of the bull's weight, was able to regain the ground he had lost. Nevertheless, he knew he couldn't run much longer.

He headed up the mountain path. Up, up he ran. Far ahead, he heard the bleating of the sheep and the snorting of the angry boar. He put on a burst of speed and reached the trees where the animals were tethered. He broke the chains of the boar and snapped the ropes binding goat and sheep. He slung the boar to the right, the goat to the left, and hurled the sheep straight ahead up the mountain path.

The three bodies of Geryon, coming up the road, saw their favorite food fleeing before them. These bodies were famished; they had never gone more than two hours without eating in their entire triple life, and, by now, they had missed three meals. And each one saw the meal it craved running away from him and was maddened by hunger. The left-hand body tried to swerve to the left after the goat; the right-hand body turned right after the pork; while the middle body tried to forge ahead after the bounding sheep.

Of course, trying to go in three different directions, they went nowhere. They stopped. They tried to run again. The more violently they moved, the less they could go. Enraged, the bodies fell upon each other. The six legs began to kick at each other's bodies. The six hands closed into fists and began to pound at the next face. The three mouths tried to fasten their fangs in each other's necks.

And, as Hercules watched from behind a tree, the three bodies of the single giant, ravaged by hunger, confused by wrath, fought savagely with themselves, and did Geryon the harm that no enemy could do. They battered faces to a pulp, kicked ribs in, and strangled themselves to death.

Geryon fell like a squashed spider and twitched in the dust.

"That was the joker in the prophecy," said Hercules. "He could be killed by no one else, as some god or demon had promised for some reason we'll never know. But split by wrath, each self hating the next self, he could be torn by a terrible inner war, and destroy himself. And I'm very happy to have thought of a way to make it happen. Now, all I have to do is swim a herd of bulls ten miles across the sea to the mainland and drive them a hundred miles to Mycenae. But that will seem easy after the work I did this afternoon ... and I'm about ready for a swim."

THE SPEAR-BIRDS
OF THE MARSH

OF ALL THE THINGS WITH WINGS IN THE WORLD OF
long ago, the Spear-birds of the Marsh were the most
dangerous. There were those who said that dragons—
which also have wings—were worse, but these people
were mistaken, because dragons always hunted alone,
while the Spear-birds did their killing in flocks.

They were very big birds, larger than eagles, with
stiltlike legs and an enormous wingspread. Their long
sharp iron beaks could break rock or pierce the strongest shield. They were always hungry and ate everything
that moved. But their favorite food was a nice juicy
human being.

To get rid of these deadly creatures was Hercules'
next task. What made it even harder was that the
Spear-birds lived in a marsh that sucked like quicksand.
Its mud swallowed everything that touched it; not even
a crocodile could live there. In fact, the only creatures

79

that could dwell in the marsh were water snakes and the Spear-birds themselves, who fed on the water snakes. Their stilt legs held them safely above the sucking mud, and their powerful wings could lift them clear when they wanted to fly away.

When Hercules came near the marsh he knew he was approaching a place of death. The edge of the swamp was littered with bones: shoulder bones and leg bones, spools of spine, rib cages, and skulls. So many kinds of skulls. Cow skulls, sheep skulls, and many human skulls with their terrible smiles. Skeleton hands held rusty shields.

Hercules studied everything very carefully. The Spear-birds were feeding. He watched them drive their long beaks deep into the mud and come out with long wriggling water snakes, which they killed by snapping them in the air like whips. He watched a bird toss the limp body in the air, catch it as it came down, and swallow it whole. He tossed a stick into the marsh to test the sucking power of the mud, and the mud swallowed the stick just as the bird had swallowed the snake.

"I can't go in there after them," he thought. "I'll have to make them come to me. But how shall I fight them? What weapons shall I use? The best way would be to make them rise in a flock and shoot my poison arrows into their midst. Yes, that's how I could kill the most of them with least danger to myself. But I would be endangering others. I would be threatening the whole countryside, for the dead birds would fall back into the marsh and their bodies, poisoned by my arrows, would poison the marsh. This huge marsh feeds a whole river system by underground streams, and the rivers would be poisoned. Cattle drinking out of these rivers would sicken and die, and people, too. No, I will not use my poison arrows, even though it would be convenient. I must think of another way. But what? If I fling a lance among them, I might hit one or two, but that's all. And to use sword or knife I'd have to bring them close enough for them to use their terrible beaks on me. Nevertheless, I do have to get them close."

He thought some more. At last he decided that the best way to fight the birds was to put on his lion-skin armor—which even those iron beaks couldn't pierce— and to stand there on the shore, letting the birds dive down at him. They would blunt their beaks against the lion hide, and he would be able to finish them off with sword or knife.

He put on the lion-skin armor, the lion-head helmet, and the great gauntlets of lion hide. He took up two of the fallen shields and clanged them together, making a hideous clattering noise. The startled birds rose in a great cloud and hovered over the marsh. Hercules danced up and down, shouting at them, beckoning to them, trying to make them attack, then stood there, sword in hand, waiting.

One of them swooped low and came at him. He took a deep breath and waited. Down, down, it came, so close that he could see its snake face and the sun flashing off its iron beak. It came closer, closer, as he crouched, waiting. The bird swerved, swooped upward. He felt the draft of air from its mighty wings, but its beak never touched him, nor did it come within reach of his hands. He watched it as it climbed away.

Another bird dived. He waited. It came closer, very

close. Then the same thing happened. When it was close enough for him to see the light splintering off its beak, it swooped up, sailed away, and joined the flock.

This happened several times. Then Hercules saw the flock coasting down. He watched the birds as they settled in the marsh again and began to feed.

"I know what it is," he said to himself. "They smell the lion skin and think I'm the lion. They've flown over Mount Nemea, these birds; it's not far from here. And a lot of them probably got killed by the lion before they learned to keep their distance. And now they won't come near me as long as I'm wearing the lion skin. But do I dare meet them uncovered? Those iron beaks will make a sieve of my body. I don't know. I have to get them close, and I can't wear the hide, so I'll have to risk it."

He cast away the lion skin, lifted the shields, clanged them again, and stood there bare-chested as the birds rose from the marsh and darkened the sky. Half-naked he stood there, watching them hover. Again he called to them and danced and beckoned. And watched a bird peel off and dive.

Hercules' breastbone was like a curved piece of brass. His own bronzed skin was tougher than leather. Between bone and skin was a great sheathing of muscle. The Spear-bird came diving so fast that Hercules had no time to swing his sword before the bird was on him, driving its beak into his chest. The beak stuck, couldn't go through.

Hercules felt a sickening pain, but the pain did not make him lose strength. His hand grasped the Spear-bird's neck and twisted the life out. The bird went limp.

But another bird was on its way and drove its beak into his chest. He chopped with the edge of his hand, breaking that bird's neck. Now two iron beaks stuck in his chest, two dead birds dangling from them. He plucked them out of his body and flung them away. Blood poured from his chest.

And the birds were coming.

One by one, they swooped down at him, stabbing with their iron beaks. The beaks bent on his massive chest, but tore the skin until the white bone showed. As they dived and stabbed, they fell into his hands, and he broke their necks. His shoulder muscles stood out in great ridges, his back muscles in great clumps, as he twisted those necks that were tougher than bull whips.

His arms were so tired now that he could hardly lift them. Dead birds were heaped about him, but there still seemed to be as many as ever hovering above. They kept diving. He was covered with blood. He knew that he had lost too much blood. He felt himself tottering. Felt his head swarm with dizziness. He knew he couldn't keep it up.

Now, he had been very careful about choosing the place to take his stand. The marsh was ringed by boulders. Beyond the boulders was a grove of pine trees. He had chosen to meet the birds at a place where one rock lay over two others, making a kind of shelter, which he had known he might need if he were losing the battle.

He needed it now. He dropped to the ground and crawled into the open cave. Just in time. As he pulled his leg under, a beak drove into the ground; a second later and he would have been nailed there with a beak through his foot. Before the bird could pull away, he

smashed its head in with a rock. Then he crouched under his boulder roof as the birds, enraged, dived at the boulder, driving their beaks against it.

To his horror, he heard the huge rock begin to crack. He had been told that the Spear-birds could crack rocks with their beaks, but he hadn't believed they could do anything against that heavy boulder. He heard them diving down at it, chipping away at it. He saw small rocks falling off like hailstones.

"By the gods," he whispered. "Another hour of this and they'll break through that boulder and I'll be like a turtle without its shell."

He saw that the low opening of his rock shelter was filling with red light, and he knew that the sun was sinking. He tried to think how long it would be before darkness fell. It was important, because these birds flew by day and roosted by night and would not keep up the attack after dark. So he crouched there listening to the boulder crumble over his head, watching the rocks slide off to make a heap of rocks, watching the red light fade, trying to think of a way to defend himself if the monster birds did break through. So busy was he measuring the light and planning what to do that he forgot about his pain and just prayed for darkness.

The red light faded, became a purple light, a black-ish-blue light, then blackness. He kept watching the boulder overhead, listening to the beaks drive into the rock. And just as the last light went, a beak did come through. But it disappeared immediately and he heard a beating of wings and felt a trickle of draft through the hole in the boulder roof. He knew that the birds were flying away into the darkness and that he was safe until dawn.

"I can't sit here," he said to himself. "I must use this night I have been given. I've got to stop this bleeding, get some strength back, and prepare for dawn. They'll be back at the first light."

He pulled oregano leaves from his pouch and chewed them into a pulp, which he then spread over his wounded chest. Chiron had taught him that the leaves of the wild mint plant called oregano had great healing power over wounds made by iron. He felt the pain draining out of his chest, felt the blood beginning to clot. But he had bled so much that he was still weak as he crawled out from under the rock and made his way into the grove of trees.

For he had a plan. It was a desperate plan, but it was the best he could do. He went among the pine trees, took vines, and braided them into a rope of vines. Then braided the ropes into a cable of vines. He found a young pine tree and bent it to the ground, then let it go. It whipped out of his hands with terrific force, snapped through its own arc, and touched the ground on the other side. He broke off a heavy branch from a fallen tree, fitted its forked end against the top of the pine, and bent the young pine again. He bent it to the ground and let it snap up. Like a giant bow it hurled the stick of wood toward the sky. Hercules bent the pine tree again, tied one of his vine cables to it, and tied the other end of the cable to the base of a nearby tree. It was a clear night, luckily, and he could see by moonlight. He found another young pine and did the same thing. He kept bending pines and tying them in a bent position until he had cocked some forty trees.

By now he was very tired. The wounds on his chest

86

had opened again and were bleeding. He chewed more oregano leaves and plastered them to his chest with great scoops of marsh mud. Now half his work was done; but he still had the other half to do, and the sky was growing pale. He had only an hour until dawn.

He raced back to his rock shelter, spread out his lion skin, and shoveled the chipped rocks onto the hide. Then he drew the four corners of the lion skin together into a great sack and swung the sack to his shoulder. It was so heavy it made him walk bowlegged, but he toiled back into the grove of trees again. One by one, he visited his bent pine trees and stuck rocks into the top branches, wedging them carefully—tightly enough so that they would not fall, but loosely enough so that they would fly out of the trees when the time came. The bent trees strained and quivered against their binding of vine as he wedged in the rocks that the Spear-birds had broken for him. But the vine cables held, and Hercules kept working until the sack was empty and the bent trees were loaded with rocks.

Now the sky was pink. He heard a loud rusty cawing as the birds settled on the marsh and began to hunt water snakes. But feeding kept them too far apart. Each bird had its own territory and drove its beak into its own space, spearing the snakes. He needed the birds in one tightly packed flock.

He picked up the two rusty shields again, stretched his arms wide, and clapped the shields together, making a horrid metallic din. The birds beat their wings, tearing their legs from the mud, rising in a great cloud out of the marsh, blotting out the pink sky.

Hercules turned and bolted toward the grove of trees.

The birds hung in the air, waiting for him to show himself. But now he was among his bent pines. He drew his knife and lashed a vine cable. The young pine whipped in an arc, loosing a storm of stones. With all the force of the springing pine behind them, the rocks hurtled more swiftly than an arrow shot from a bow or a stone flung from a sling and swept through the flock in a murderous hail.

Birds dropped. Hercules watched them fall. He yelled for joy and sprang from tree to tree, slashing vines. The trees whipped up, loosing their hail of stones, sending them among the flock. The flock broke. Single birds began to scoot away. None dived.

The pink sky was yellow now, a glorious full dawn. The marsh was free of birds. Dead birds lay among the bones of the creatures they had killed, and soon their bones would be added to the rubble.

Hercules was very weary. He had lost much blood. But he had scattered the flock and killed most of the Spear-birds. It would be a long time before they could terrorize the countryside again. He picked up his lion skin and his weapons and limped away from the marsh, heading for a river where he could swim and cleanse himself.

"Then," he thought, "I'll sleep for the rest of the day and all tonight. And tomorrow I'll set out, but not for Mycenae. No, I've earned a bit of rest. I shall go to Thebes and see my parents and tell Iole the story of my adventures."

THE OLD MAN
OF THE SEA

ᒪᒪᒪᒪᒪᒪᒪᒪᒪᒪᒪᒪᒪᒪᒪᒪᒪᒪᒪᒪᒪᒪᒪᒪᒪᒪᒪᒪᒪ

IN THOSE DAYS, EVERYONE KNEW THAT THE EARTH WAS flat and that the sky was held up by mountains. But at the very northwestern corner of the world, in the uttermost island behind the West Wind, that part of the sky was held up by a Titan named Atlas, who did a mountain's work. He was there because in the beginning of time he had fought against Zeus, and it was his punishment to stand in that orchard forever holding the sky on his shoulders.

The place he stood was called the Garden of the Hesperides, but it was more of an orchard than a garden. Apple trees grew in that orchard, and one tree bore apples of solid gold. This tree had not always been there. It was Mother Earth's wedding gift to Hera and had been planted in the Garden of the Gods on Olympus. Hera had been very selfish about these apples and would never give any to the other gods, who, after a while, began to help themselves. So she dug up her tree, took it as far as she could—to the western edge of the world—and replanted it in the orchard there. And to make sure that the fruit would not be stolen, she set a giant serpent to guard the tree. It wound itself around the trunk and devoured anyone who came near.

To fetch one of these golden apples from the dangerous orchard on the western rim of the world, where the Titan, Atlas, held the sky on his shoulders, became the next task facing Hercules.

Hercules was given this message as he stood before the iron gates of Mycenae, and again it was Copreus who brought him the king's commands.

"I'll need some directions, my friend," said Hercules. "Everyone has heard of this tree and these apples, but no one seems to know how to get there."

"Only one creature in the world can tell you that," said Copreus. "The Old Man of the Sea alone knows the secret of the orchard."

"And where do I find him?"

"He dwells on the island of Ner, which is his kingdom. His own name is Nereus, but he is known as the Old Man of the Sea. And I must warn you: he's a pretty unpleasant sort of fellow. Not at all easy to deal with."

"I'm getting used to that," said Hercules. "Everything about these missions gets unpleasant sooner or later. Farewell."

Hercules, as usual, felt very much alone in the world as he set out on his mission. But this time he was less alone. For someone else was also thinking very hard about the Old Man of the Sea. It happened this way.

After leaving Thebes, Iole and the Blind Man had

wandered here and there for many months and had at last reached a wild and lonely beach, where they decided to stay. They built a little driftwood shack and lived there. The Blind Man spent hours telling her stories, and the more he told, the more she wanted to hear. She loved his stories. He also taught her to play the lyre, which he played beautifully. Often, in the evening, they would sit on a rock at the very edge of the sea, and he would touch the strings and sing a story-song. The fish would come to the surface and bob in the swell, listening.

Iole made friends with these music-loving fish, especially a dolphin, because the Blind Man had known him a long time and had taught the dolphin to speak. But the man was not easy to live with. Sometimes a mood would come on him, and he would sit on his rock all day from dawn to dusk, gazing out at the sea, refusing to eat, not speaking a word. And would sit there all night, too, without sleeping, his milky eyes looking out into the darkness of the waters. Then, Iole knew, the next dawn he would be choking with visions and gasp out strange words. These words would dance upon the air and form a picture of what was to be.

She stayed close to him on such dawns, although he didn't seem to know whether she was there or not. But she always listened thirstily to his prophecies, for she knew that they were very important to her without knowing why. Upon this dawn, he arose suddenly from his rock, stretched his arms to the rising sun, and cried, "The apples, the golden apples! The eight-armed fish, the lobster-faced liar, beware, beware . . . He's a liar, Hercules, beware, beware . . ."

Iole saw him sway on his feet. His arms dropped. She leaped to him and flung her arm around his waist, easing him to the sand, where he lay insensible. This had happened before, and she knew what to do. She dragged him up on the beach beyond the high-tide mark, fetched a blanket from the shack to cover him with, and set some lentil soup to boil. For he would awake very hungry, she knew, and could not be questioned about his words until he had eaten. And she had to question him very closely, for this prophecy concerned Hercules.

He woke up after a few hours and ate his soup greedily. Then Iole asked him about the words he had spoken out of his trance.

"What do they mean, Grandfather?"

He sat there silently.

"Tell me. Please . . ."

"I'd rather not."

"It's about Hercules."

"That's why. What I saw in my darkness will grieve you."

"It won't. I mean, he's always fighting monsters. Whatever he's doing now can't be worse than what he's done before. What is the eight-armed fish?"

"An octopus. A giant one. One which has killed and eaten a great white shark."

"What has it to do with Hercules?"

"This octopus guards an island called Ner, where dwells one named Nereus, known as the Old Man of the Sea. And Hercules is coming to visit him. Now, one of two things will happen, and I don't know which is worse. Either Hercules will be devoured by the octopus, or he will reach the island and question Nereus, who will give him a fatal answer."

"What will he ask Nereus?"

"Hercules' task is to fetch a golden apple from the Garden of the Hesperides. Only Nereus knows the secret of that orchard—how to find it, and how to pick the apples."

"And he's a liar, isn't he? You called him a lobster-faced liar."

"He is that. He has been bribed by King Eurystheus to tell Hercules exactly the wrong way to go about things, a way that will get him killed in the shortest possible time. Don't cry."

"I'm not crying, I'm thinking. I fear the liar more than the octopus. I've seen Hercules fight the Hydra, and I know what he can do, although he fights better on land than in the water. But he's so honest himself that he doesn't understand about lies and liars. He'll believe Nereus. He must be warned."

"How can he be warned? He sails toward Ner now; I've seen him sailing upon the waters of sleep."

"I shall warn him. Good-by, Grandfather."

Before he could say anything, she hugged him, kissed his blind eyes, and flashed away. She ran to the edge of the beach, shouting and singing. Her voice mixed with the wind and the seething of the waves. A dolphin breached in a glittering arc, slid into the water again, and stuck its head out near her.

"You have called?"

"I have called, and you have come." She leaped onto his back.

"Do you want a ride?"

"A long ride—to the island of Ner."

The dolphin stopped swimming. He turned his head back to look at Iole, who was riding him astride, as though he were a horse. "Dearest girl," he said, "the sea holds many dreadful creatures, and there are few that I fear. I have fought off killer whales, slid through the coils of sea serpents, and will dare them again if I must. But the one creature I fear is the giant octopus that guards the island of Ner."

"But I've adopted you as my best friend and my water steed," said Iole. "If you won't take me there, I can't go. And I must."

"Why?"

She told him about what the Blind Man had seen, about Hercules and the golden apples, and Nereus, and how she had to warn Hercules about the lies that would be told by the Old Man of the Sea.

"But why should he wish to harm Hercules?"

"He has been bribed by the king of Mycenae, who hates Hercules and is always trying to destroy him."

"I see. And do you know how the king would have bribed the Old Man of the Sea? What he values most is food for his octopus. And that monster's favorite food is a child. The king would have promised to send Nereus a shipload of slave children to feed the octopus. If you go to that island—that is, if I can get you safely past the octopus—why, then Nereus will catch you and toss you right back into the monster's jaws. Don't risk it, I beg you."

"I must go. Will you take me?"

"If you must go, I suppose I must take you."

The island of Ner was too far, Hercules thought, to

reach by swimming. He chopped down a tree, trimmed it of branches, cut it into logs, and lashed them together with vines. Then he stuck his spear into the raft so that it stood upright, making a tall mast, and hung his lion skin as a sail. He attached a heavy flat piece of wood to the stern of his raft as a steering oar and set sail. An east wind bore him westward, which was the way he wanted to go. In two days he came to the island of Ner. It was girded by rocks, and he sailed around the island looking for a way through.

He heard a curious slithering sound. Before his amazed eyes something grew out of the water. He thought it was a snake, then saw it wasn't. It groped toward the raft; he saw that it had a rubbery tip that could curl like a hand. It slid onto the raft and tried to grasp a log. He raised his foot and stamped on it with his heel. It whisked away. But then another one came, and then another long snaky arm. In the frothing water he saw a great round thing, and many other wavering arms. The raft began to rock violently, and he realized that he was being attacked by a giant octopus. His raft was long and broad; he had lashed many logs together. It was a huge platform of logs and was very hard to overturn. Had it been a skiff or even a larger ship, the octopus would have tipped it over like a wine cup. But the raft would not capsize; it tilted violently, but held. Hercules kept stamping on the rubbery arms, feeling the logs splinter under his feet as he stamped, but balancing himself on the pitching raft.

He knew he couldn't keep it up. The raft was tilting too steeply. He knew he would have to slide off and fight in the water where he would be at the monster's mercy. He leaped to the spear which was his mast,

wrenched it out of the log, and jabbed mightily, punching holes in three of the arms. Now the raft was slippery with blood. Now five arms were sweeping over the logs, and to his horror, he saw the poached eyes and horny beak of the octopus, hoisting itself on board. Swiftly, he donned the lion skin. In that moment of utmost peril, his mind went back, back, to when he had been a baby in a bull-hide cradle and the serpents had come at him. These octopus arms hugging him now were like serpents. They could not crush him in his lion skin, but he knew that the octopus would hug him tight, fall into the water with him, hold him under till he drowned, and eat him at its leisure.

But now his big powerful hands were doing what his baby hands had done so long ago. He seized two of the arms and tied them together in a double knot. He stooped suddenly, caught two other arms, and knotted them together. Working swiftly, swiftly, straining every muscle, wrestling the enormous sea beast, falling backward under the hard blubbery mass, he took its full weight on his chest and ribs, bracing himself so that he would not be crushed. He felt the terrible beak hammering against the lion hide; nevertheless, his hands kept working, and two by two he tied the arms together so that they could not move.

He rose suddenly. The beast crashed to the logs, splintering them. Hercules cast off his lion skin, stooped, lifted the huge knotted octopus, holding the beaked mouth away from him, and threw the monster into the sea. He watched it sink. With its legs tied it could not swim. It sank to the bottom. Its brutish little brain could not think with its legs tied. When it grasped something, it always ate. Now all its legs were grasping something. It was grasping itself. Its spark of intelligence turned to utter greed, and it began to eat itself. It ate itself all up until only the mouth was left. Then that swallowed itself.

Hercules was in the water now. His raft was a wreckage of logs. He draped his lion skin over two of the logs that were still bound together, sat astride them, and poled himself toward shore with his spear. He threaded his way through the rocks, fending them off with his spear, poling himself in by main strength until he was in shallow water and could wade ashore.

It was dark now; he knew he had better wait until morning before he hunted for Nereus. He lay down and fell fast asleep, and was still sleeping when dawn began to smolder in the sky. He was unaware that Iole had come to the island riding on the dolphin.

Iole slid off the dolphin's back, kissed his nose, and said, "Farewell, my friend."

"You might want to get off this island fast," said the dolphin. "If you need me, just sing out. I'll be somewhere offshore."

"Thank you," said Iole.

She kissed him again, and he whisked out of sight. She didn't exactly know what to do now that she was on the island. She couldn't do anything until Hercules came. Then she had to get to him and warn him to believe nothing the Old Man of the Sea might say.

"But what will I do if that horrid thing finds me first?" she thought. "I'd better hide. Where, though? And I'm so hungry."

She searched for a berry bush, found one, and began to eat. The berries were very sour, but there was nothing else. She ate a handful and was just finishing when she heard something howl.

She climbed a tree. Then saw something coming that almost made her heart stop beating. Nereus was shambling along the beach. She knew it must be he because the Blind Man had said something about a "lobster-face," and there couldn't be two creatures in the world so ugly. Nereus was the only son of the Lobster Queen and a fisherman she had caught, and, unfortunately, he looked more like his mother. His upper body was that of a scaly old man, but he had a lobster face with antennae and stalked eyes. His hands were enormous lobster claws, and he had webbed feet.

As we know, Iole was a very brave girl, but this thing was too gruesome. She opened her eyes and looked at him and quickly closed them again. He was prowling along the beach. Occasionally, he dug in the sand with his claw, plucked out a clam, and crunched it, shell and all. Once in a while, he looked out to sea and howled for his octopus; he liked to see it now and then, just to know it was there.

"Oh my," thought Iole, "that creepy crawly thing doesn't even have to try to kill me. If he ever touches me with one of those horrid claws, I'll curl up and die. But where can I hide? Not here. I'm sure he can climb trees. I'd better find a cave or a cleft in the rocks anyway."

Suddenly he turned and came toward her. She held her breath. He stopped and listened, his stalked eyes veering and tipping, looking up once, it seemed, into the branches of Iole's tree. She had to let out her breath but didn't dare to. He walked away.

She waited for a while after he had disappeared around a bend of the beach, then crept down the tree and went along the shore. It was littered with rocks, large and small, but it was a flat place, and there were no caves as such. She did find a deep cleft in the rocks that looked wide enough for her to get into and deep enough to hide in.

"This will have to do," she thought. "But I'm liable to wait a long time before Hercules comes; I'd better get some more berries and take them in with me."

She ran back to the bush, tore a piece off her tunic, and filled the rag with berries. Just as she was tying it into a sack, she heard a howling. She whirled, and saw Nereus scuttling toward her. She flashed away. He came with amazing speed on those webbed feet. He almost caught her. One claw actually did catch a bit of her hair that was whipping behind her as she ran. Her horror became speed. She reached the cleft in the rocks and dived in just as he stretched his arm for her, clacking his claws. She ducked, and the pincers clattered over her head. She shrank deeper into the cleft, as far as she could go. She knew Nereus could see her because she could see him, dancing with rage.

"Come out!" he howled. "Come out immediately! My octopus is very hungry. You're not fat enough for a real meal but you'll make a nice snack, so come out."

"Oh, Hercules," she said to herself, "how I wish you were here."

She said it like a prayer, but unlike most prayers, it was answered immediately. She heard a beloved golden voice bawling: "Ho there, old fellow, I need a word with you." And peering through the rocks, she saw a pair of tall bronzed legs planted on the sand. Through all her grief and fear she hadn't allowed herself to weep, but now she wept tears of pure joy. She saw Nereus turn away from the cleft, and she crawled up closer to hear what was being said:

"You there," said Hercules. "Stop that howling. I want to ask you something."

Nereus turned, snarling. But when he saw a giant youth standing before him, twirling an enormous spear in one hand, he tried to change his snarl into a smile and looked uglier than ever.

"I beg your pardon, young man," he said, "but I've been busy with a very naughty little girl who's refusing to feed a poor starving octopus."

"He's just eaten," said Hercules. "Tell me, where can I find Nereus, otherwise known as the Old Man of the Sea?"

"You've found him. That's me."

"Then please tell me how to find the Garden of the Hesperides where grow the golden apples."

"Gladly shall I tell you how to reach that secret place."

"And how to pick the apples, and what dangers to avoid?"

"Gladly, gladly."

"Well, start talking, my fishy friend."

"You must guide yourself by this verse:

> Honey to the snake.
> Titan's burden take . . .
> To prove the giant's worth,
> Stretch him flat on earth . . ."

"I don't understand."

"Well, it's a magical verse and full of riddles. You'll have to solve it for yourself."

101

Hercules picked up Nereus by the scruff of the neck and dangled him high over the rock. "Riddle me no riddles, lobster-face, or I'll break you into bite-sized pieces and feed you to the gulls."

"Gently, dear sir. I was just about to say that in your case, perhaps, plain words are best."

"Much the best," growled Hercules.

"Won't you put me down?"

"When you tell me plainly what I want to know."

"I could speak much more comfortably if I were on my feet again."

"You don't know what discomfort means yet. But you will if you don't start talking."

"Well, this is the meaning of the first line. Wrapped about the trunk of Hera's apple tree is an enormous serpent named Ladon. He is there to keep off thieves and will certainly make a meal of you unless you buy him off."

"How?"

"With honey. This Ladon has the sweetest tooth ever known, ninety-six of the sweetest teeth, in fact. If you give him enough honeycombs to munch, he'll be so happy eating them he'll let you walk away with all the apples you want. That's the meaning of the first line, 'Honey to the snake.' As for the second line, 'Titan's burden take . . .' you must know that Atlas, eldest of the Titans, once was foolish enough to rebel against Zeus, and as punishment he has to bear that part of the sky on his shoulders. Now he's been there for many many centuries and is very weary of his task. He may ask you to take his place for a while. If you agree to help him, he'll let you steal some apples, for part of his duties is to guard them also."

"What do the other lines mean?"

"Please set me down. I'm getting dizzy."

Hercules shook him slightly. "Keep talking. There are worse things than dizziness."

"Yes, yes. Third and fourth lines: 'To prove the giant's worth,/stretch him flat on earth.' Before you return you will have to wrestle the giant, Anteus. Now, he's an awful creature to have to wrestle. Tall as a cedar he is, ten times your own height. And so wide that he looks squat. But he has one weakness, and if you know what it is, you may save yourself. He hates the memory of his own childhood and can't bear any contact with his mother."

Hercules' fingers tightened around the scaly throat. "More riddles?"

"Aaagh. Loosen your fingers, man! I can't tell you anything if you strangle me."

Hercules eased his grip.

"Thank you, thank you," moaned Nereus. "I meant no riddles, believe me. By 'his mother,' I mean Mother Earth. Anteus, mightiest wrestler in the world, has this one weak spot: if you lay him flat on the ground, he loses all his strength and becomes as helpless as an infant. That's what those lines mean: 'To prove the giant's worth,/stretch him flat on earth.' Lay him flat on the ground, if you can, and he'll lose all his strength. So that's the secret. Three secrets, in fact. I've unlocked the riddle of the verse and given you the information you need to take the apples and get yourself back alive. So now you owe me something."

"Well, I like to pay my debts. What can I do?"

"See that selfish girl hiding in there? Please pry her out of those rocks."

103

Still holding the Old Man of the Sea, Hercules picked up the huge boulder and tossed it away like a pebble. He lifted the girl and brought her face to face with Nereus.

"Oh, Hercules," she whispered. "I'm so glad you've come . . ."

"Iole! Dear dear girl, what are you doing here?"

"I came to warn you against him. He's a liar. He's been paid to lie to you. Whatever he told you, you've got to do the opposite."

"No, she's lying," whimpered Nereus. "She's lying faster than she can talk. Wicked wicked wicked girl! Are you trying to get me killed? Take it back! Please . . ."

"Sounds like the truth to me," said Hercules.

"No, Hercules, no!" cried Nereus. "She's just trying to get me in trouble."

"She's succeeding."

"No, no. Please listen . . ."

"I listened to you before, didn't I? And you chose to tell me lies."

"I didn't, I didn't. I'm so honest, it's unbelievable. Let me go, and I'll give you a bushel of pearls."

"Too generous, Nereus."

Lifting his arm high, he slammed Nereus feet first into a flat rock with such force that the Old Man of the Sea was driven into the rock like a nail into soft wood. But he was immortal for all his ugliness, so he could not die, although driven so deeply into the rock that only his mouth remained unburied. And his lips opened and closed, sucking little creatures from the tide, the first sea anemone.

Hercules was left holding Iole, who was looking up at him, smiling through her tears.

"Your face is dirty," he said gently.

"Put me down."

He set her on the ground. She raced down the beach to a tidal pool and washed her tear-stained face. Then Hercules sat on a rock. She snuggled in his lap, and he stroked her hair.

"How did you know about Nereus?" he said. "And how did you get here?"

Sitting there under the morning sun with her head against his shoulder, she told him all about the Blind Man, and how she had left Thebes and wandered with the old prophet, and what he had seen in the vision, and how she had ridden the dolphin to the island of Ner to warn Hercules. She also told him that she had decided not to marry him after all.

"That may be just as well," said Hercules. "I think I've promised to marry someone else."

"Who?"

"A princess named Dienera. Her father is king of Calydon."

"Why did you? What's she like? Where did you meet her?"

He told her about his fight with the river and cleaning the Augean stables.

"You don't have to marry her just because you saved her, you know. Do you love her?"

"Well, she asked me that too, and I told her I didn't know. She says it doesn't matter because she loves me enough for both of us."

"That's nonsense, of course."

"Perhaps, but she began to cry, and the only way I could make her stop was by promising to marry her."

"How about your promise to me?"

"You're not old enough yet."

"I'm growing fast. Don't you notice how much taller I am?"

"Yes."

"So you've got to break your promise to me or to her. You promised me first."

"Didn't you just tell me you'd changed your mind about the whole thing?"

"Well, I might change it again. I have time before I'm old enough."

"But she's old enough now, you see. And when I tell her anything she doesn't want to hear, she starts to cry."

"I can cry too, you know."

"But you won't, will you? You're my brave girl who saved me from the Hydra and came here to save me from the lies of Nereus. You're the bravest smartest girl in the world; you're no cry-baby."

"That doesn't mean I can't feel just as sad as that weepy princess. Maybe even sadder."

"How about my brother, Iphicles. He'll wait for you if I ask him. He's a good little chap."

"I don't like little chaps. I like them exactly your size."

"He'll be king of Thebes one day. Wouldn't you like to be queen?"

"Not a bit—unless you're the king."

"Oh no, I wouldn't be any good as a king. I don't like to tell people what to do."

"Let Dienera marry your brother. She sounds like she'd enjoy being queen."

"Say, that's not a bad idea. I'll discuss it with her as soon as I get back with the apples."

"Don't tell her it's *my* idea. Tell her Iphicles has fallen

madly in love with her and can't eat and can't sleep because he's thinking of her all the time. And that he has
asked you to find out if she prefers diamonds or rubies
or emeralds, or all three combined."

"That doesn't sound like Iphicles."

"What's the difference? She won't know that. You
just tell her exactly what I told you, word for word."

"I'll never remember it all."

"I'll write it down for you, and you must memorize it.
You don't really want to marry her and make me very
sad, do you?"

"Truth is, I'm not ready to be anybody's husband
yet. I have too much fighting left to do."

"Absolutely. And in a few years you'll have wiped
out all the monsters in the world and be ready for other
things."

"Unless one of them wipes me out first."

"I suppose you won't take me with you to the Garden
of the Hesperides?"

"No, Iole dear. I can't take you there."

"Good-by then. Remember, do everything just the
opposite of what Nereus said."

She waded out into the surf, whistling. The dolphin
slid in on a wave, and Hercules watched as she mounted
the creature and rode away toward the horizon.

HADES ASKS FOR HELP

ᎶᎶᎶᎶᎶᎶᎶᎶᎶᎶᎶᎶᎶᎶᎶᎶᎶᎶᎶᎶᎶᎶᎶ

HADES, RULER OF THE DEAD, WAS IN A BAD MOOD.
His demons had just taken a ghost count in the Land beyond Death and had told him what he did not want to
hear: his kingdom was not growing as fast as it should.
He decided he'd better do something about this and set
up a meeting with his brother, Poseidon, god of the
sea; his nephew Ares, god of war; and his sister, Hera.

It was to be a secret meeting, because he didn't want
Zeus to know anything about his plans. So they
couldn't meet on Olympus, and his own kingdom, Tartarus, was too gloomy; no one wanted to go there. But
Poseidon invited them to meet in one of his undersea
grottoes, where Zeus couldn't see them, and where they
would be served a delicious seafood dinner by green-
haired water nymphs.

They met in the great grotto, which had glass walls so
that they could see the giant turtles, the octopi, the

gliding sharks, the blind slugs, and all the curious creatures which dwell at the bottom of the sea. The chamber was full of filtered green light and was very quiet.

"Sister, brother, nephew," said Hades, "I need your help. My kingdom isn't growing fast enough. People are living too long. We just can't depend on natural causes any more. So the favor I must ask divides itself into three favors.

"You, brother Poseidon, please whistle up some dreadful storms, not just the kind that wreck a few ships here and there, but real killers, you know. Enormous tempests, hurricanes, typhoons—the kind that blow whole cities away. Tidal waves that will wash over an entire island, drowning everybody. A month or two of such weather will do wonders for me . . .

"You, Ares, you know, of course, what I want you to do. There's been much too much peace lately. It's breaking out everywhere. Go down with sword and shield and plant the seeds of hatred. Make people fear each other, make them attack each other. Not just private duels—I want you to hurl whole nations against each other. Tell lies, start rumors, go from one side of a border to the other, any border, killing people on both sides, so each country will blame the other for the murders. Then plant the idea of huge armies in the minds of kings, and since big armies can't just sit at home eating their heads off, they will be sent to attack each other, and we shall have our wars, bloody ones, with fields full of corpses and shoals of souls to fatten my realm. Between your fire storms and Poseidon's water storms, hell will prosper again."

"I'll be glad to do what I can," said Ares.

"What you have asked me will mean a lot of bother," said Poseidon, "but I know you will help me when I need it, so I agree."

"Why have you called me here?" said Hera. "I am queen of the gods, it is true, but I can do nothing that Zeus would object to. And he would dislike this plan of yours very much, Hades. For some reason, I don't know why, he likes that pesky race called humankind and seeks to protect them from harm."

"Sister and queen," said Hades, "I know that you do not share your husband's strange affection for humankind. Nevertheless, without meaning to, you have been helping him help them."

"What do you mean?"

"In your hatred of that gigantic young Hercules, you set him to fighting monsters all over the world. I know that your intentions have been good, I know that you have wanted to destroy him, but instead he's been destroying these monsters. And for every monster that he kills, he is saving thousands of people, whom the monsters used to devour. So far, he's wiped out the Nemean Lion, the Hydra, the three-bodied Geryon, and a flock of Spear-birds."

"Not to mention two of my finest sea serpents," grumbled Poseidon.

"He's been very lucky, so far," said Hera. "I have no doubt that Zeus has been giving him secret help. I can't prove it, but it must be so."

"Whatever the reason, dear sister, you simply must kill him before he kills any more monsters and saves any more people."

"He's on a journey now," said Hera. "And this one

should really finish him off. He's trying to steal golden apples from the Garden of the Hesperides. Now, my tree there is guarded by a giant serpent named Ladon, an enormous thing, dear Poseidon, which makes your two serpents look like earthworms. If, by any chance, he should escape Ladon, then Atlas will get him. Hercules is big, but he's no match for the mountain-sized Atlas, whose temper is very short, because he's tired of holding up the sky. And if, by some miracle, he should escape Atlas also, there is another fearsome giant awaiting him in Libya. But I don't think he'll get that far."

"Terrible creatures, you describe," said Hades. "But the Nemean Lion and the Hydra and the octopus were supposed to be deadly, too, and you know what he did to them. What I'm asking, dear Hera, is for you, personally, to make sure he dies before the month is out."

"I can't kill him myself," said Hera. "Zeus would find out and would punish me very painfully. I'll have to do it through someone else."

"Well, get someone intelligent, not a stupid monster," said Hades. "Use someone he won't suspect. Do it by treachery. And supervise every step of the murder yourself."

"Brother," said Hera, "one way or other, Hercules shall die before the month is out. Upon my oath as queen of the gods, it shall be done."

"Farewell, I'm off to start some wars," said Ares.

"As soon as you're gone, I'll see about those tempests and tidal waves and things," said Poseidon.

"Brother, sister, nephew," said Hades, "I thank you all. Do your worst, that's all anyone can ask."

THE GOLDEN APPLES

IT WAS A HILLY ISLAND. MEADOWS RAN RIGHT DOWN TO the water's edge. Deer and wild horses came down to the sea to swim. Towering above all was Atlas, snow-bearded, with huge misty eyes, holding the sky on his shoulders. If you didn't know about the Titan, you would think he was a mountain.

Fruit trees grew thickly in the orchard, and Hercules searched for a long time before he saw the golden apples flashing among dark green leaves. He came closer, stepping carefully, waiting for the serpent to show itself. Then he saw it and stood there, amazed.

He had heard that Ladon would be wrapped around the tree trunk, but the serpent had unwrapped itself and was coiled in front of the tree. It raised its head as Hercules came near—at least, he thought it must be its head because he saw two eyes. Otherwise, the serpent's body ran right into its head; its jaws were hinged at the

114

tail. In other words, Ladon was a quarter-mile of living mouth lined with teeth.

"Well," said Hercules to himself, "how in the world am I expected to get past that monster? What did Nereus say? 'Honey to the snake.' But everything he said was a lie, wasn't it? And it doesn't really seem that I could buy off this beast with a dab of honey. What shall I do, though? He's too big to strangle. No blade will pierce that leather hide. I can't use my poison arrows and spoil all the fruit of the orchard and poison the rivers and streams of this beautiful island. 'Honey to the snake.' Nereus was a liar, but the best liars always throw in a tiny bit of truth to make their lies sound good. Honeycomb, bees . . . Perhaps I'm getting an idea."

He backed away from the serpent and angled off into the woods searching for a dead tree. He reached in and pulled out a beehive and hung it from his belt. The bees buzzed angrily. They swarmed out in a black cloud and settled on his chest and shoulders, stabbing with their stingers. But his skin was too tough; the stingers broke off. The bees crept back into their hive. He searched for other hollow trees. When he came back to the orchard, his belt was hung with buzzing cones.

He walked slowly toward Hera's tree. The serpent saw him and opened its jaws. Hercules was looking right down a quarter-mile of pink and black gullet set with ivory knives. The jaws slithered toward him. He took a hive from his belt and, aiming carefully, threw it straight into the jaws, through the hedge of teeth, and saw it travel down the gullet to the jaw hinge at the serpent's tail.

One by one, he pulled the hives from his belt and hurled them into the yawning gullet. The serpent, drunk on the smell of honey, closed its jaws. But it wasn't only combs being crunched. The bees were in there too, and bees make a peppery dish. They swarmed out and thrust the wicked little hooks of their tails into the serpent's palate, the only place on its body not covered by leather hide. It was like eating fire.

In instant agony, Ladon uncoiled with the force of a thousand steel springs. High, high into the air went the serpent, tail flailing. Hercules held his oak-tree club, waiting. The serpent turned in the air and came plunging down at him. He swung his great club, smashing it into Ladon's body, splitting it open, shattering its fangs. Bits of ivory and honeycomb rained down on the meadow, and the body of the serpent, squashed like an earthworm by a gardener's spade, fell into the sea and sank out of sight.

Hercules walked toward Hera's tree. He reached for an apple. Thunder spoke out of the clear sky.

"Stop, thief!"

He dropped his hand. He knew it must be Atlas speaking, and he remembered that he would have to meet the Titan before he could take the apples. He walked through the orchard and made his way to the other side of the island where Atlas stood. Here he saw the heavy blue bowl of the sky pressing on the shoulders of the Titan. He stood at the giant feet and looked up, up toward the snowy beard and the vast misty eyes. He heard the voice rumble again.

"Off with you, little thief, before I start an avalanche and bury you under a ton of rock."

116

"I'm no thief," said the young man. "I do not steal. I take. I am Hercules."

"Why didn't you say so in the first place? I've been waiting for you. I've been standing here for a thousand years, waiting."

"Waiting for what?"

"For someone strong enough to hold up my part of the sky while I take a little rest. The name they spoke was Hercules."

" 'They' are mistaken, whoever 'they' are," said Hercules. "I haven't come here to hold up any sky, but to pick some apples."

"One little stamp of my foot and a ton of rocks will roll down on you," said Atlas. "So you won't get very far with your apples."

Indeed, just at that moment, a huge boulder came rolling down the slope of the Titan's thigh. Hercules had to leap away or he would have been crushed beneath it.

"That was just a sample," said Atlas.

"All right," called Hercules. "I'll make a bargain with you. If you let me have an apple or two, I'll take your place for a little while."

"I agree. I agree. Take the sky."

"But only for a very short while. I'm supposed to be strong for a human being, but I'm no Titan, you know. If I take the sky from you, you must take it back quickly."

"Agreed, agreed," said Atlas. "Are you going to stand there talking about it for another thousand years? Climb to the top of that hill there, and I'll pass you the sky."

Hercules climbed to the top of a nearby hill and called out, "Before I take it, just tell me in plain words how long you'll be."

"Not long, not long. I just want to stretch my legs a bit. I'll run across to that orchard, pick your apples, and come back."

"Do you promise?"

"Upon my word as a Titan—Titans are older than the gods and much more honest."

And Atlas, moving swiftly for something so large, lifted the bowl of the sky from his shoulders and set its rim on the shoulders of Hercules. His knees sagged. He felt them sagging. He felt his spine crumbling. But he couldn't bear to show any weakness. Pride became a steel rod running from his soles to the top of his head, stiffening his backbone. His knees locked. Thighs and legs bunched like rock, welding him to the mountain top. He stood there, hunched, muscles writhing, stood there on the mountain top holding the sky on his shoulders.

Atlas skipped over the island, trampling trees and blowing eagle nests out of the cliffs with the wind of his laughter.

Hercules stood, waiting. His shoulders were on fire. He felt his ribs caving in. He could hardly turn his head. He rolled his eyes, searching for the Titan. The light faded. He felt the sinking sun warm his back, saw his own hunched shadow on the plain below. It was a sight he didn't want to see.

"Atlas," he called. "Atlas!"

A thunderous chuckle rolled across the valley.

"Atlas! Where are you? Come back!"

Thunder chuckled again. "Little fool, I'll never come back."

"You promised."

"I lied."

Hercules, with great effort, moved his head, shifting his gaze upward. The evening star had come out. It is the first star to burn in the western sky. He looked deep into its greenish blue light; it seemed to be laughing at him. He shrugged. And the star fell hissing into the sea, starting a plume of steam and leaving a scar of light in the sky.

"Hold still!" roared Atlas. "If you move, the stars will fall, and we will burn, burn . . ."

"I can't help moving," said Hercules. "My shoulders are sore."

"Never mind pain. It's only for eternity. Bear your burden like a man."

"I'll do my best," said Hercules. "But I'll need a pad of some kind. My lion pelt will do. If I can fold it on my shoulders under the edge of the sky, then I'll be able to stand here forever and not twitch or shake the stars."

"Very well," said Atlas. "Use your pelt."

"But you must hold the sky for a bit, while I fold the pelt on my shoulders."

"Oh, no," said Atlas. "Out of the question. Never again will I hold that sky."

Hercules shrugged. The horn of the moon snapped off and the tide, feeling its silver reins loosen, sprang upon the beach. Atlas found himself knee-deep in water. It swirled higher and higher.

"Clumsy little idiot!" he bellowed. "Miserable weakling! You cracked the moon and unbound the tides."

120

"My shoulders are getting sorer and sorer," said Hercules. "And look, there are more stars out now. They'll be raining down in a minute. Better let me fix that pad."

He saw Atlas wading toward him.

"All right, all right," called the Titan. "I'll hold that accursed sky again, but just for a second. Then you must take it back and bear it forever."

"I promise," said Hercules.

Atlas groaned, hunching his back again under the awful weight of the sky. Hercules, feeling light as a feather and full of joy, raced down the slope of the mountain and splashed through the shrinking tide to where the apple tree stood. He filled his pouch with the golden fruit.

"Stop! Stop! What are you doing?" cried Atlas.

"Breaking the same promise you did. Taking a few apples."

Atlas lifted his gigantic foot, preparing to stamp, and to start an avalanche that would bury Hercules under a ton of rock. But the stars were still wobbling and began to rain spears of fire. And Atlas had to steady himself quickly and quiet the sky. For in the beginning of the world, all the gods had helped adorn the heavens and were very proud of their great chandelier of stars. He did not dare let it break.

"Farewell," called Hercules. "Don't think badly of me. I, too, have burdens which I can't pass on to anyone else."

Atlas didn't answer. He was weeping. His tears were snowflakes, the first of that year.

ZEUS LOOKS DOWN

DEEP DOWN BENEATH THE EARTH, IN THE VERY DEPTHS of Tartarus, Hades sat on his ivory and ebony throne watching the hordes of the newly dead passing before him driven by demons. Hades was so happy, he almost smiled, for he was getting the help he asked for, and his kingdom was growing and growing.

Poseidon prowled the waters of the world. He whistled up the four winds and sent them rampaging across the sea, sinking ships and drowning their crews. He whipped the winds into a wild circular dance, which became tempest and hurricane, sweeping away forests, farms, entire cities. He quaked the bottom of the sea, splashing up a huge tidal wave that swept over the islands, drowning everyone.

And on fair days, when the weather wasn't killing them, men were killing each other. Ares had come to earth to kindle hatred in the hearts of men, and the nations of the world hurled armies against each other. With spear and arrow they attacked each other, with fire and sword and flung stone. The beaked ships of their navies rammed great holes in each other; sailors were flung into the water and eaten by sharks.

Finally, the sounds of anger and grief and terror reached even to heaven, and Zeus, sitting on Olympus, heard the clamor. He looked down, and what he saw made him very sad. He couldn't understand what was happening below. He called his daughter, Athene, goddess of wisdom.

"Why is mankind behaving this way?" he said. "Why are they killing each other?"

"They are following our example and dancing to our tune."

"What do you mean?"

"When they kill, they copy us. When Poseidon whistles a typhoon out of a clear sky and sweeps away their homes, they know that the god of the sea is a killer; his weapon is storm. And they have been told that whatever gods do is good."

"You can't blame their wars on Poseidon."

"I can blame Ares. He has planted the seeds of hatred in their hearts. He has stuffed the minds of foolish kings with the idea that their safety depends on the number of corpses they can produce and the amount of treasure they can steal from one another. So they raise armies and make war. O Father, if we really want to know why humankind is bloodthirsty, we should look at ourselves."

"What do you suggest, O wise maiden?"

"We gods are very mighty; our faults are mighty, too.

123

We're all related and share the same bad habits. We have known absolute power, and that rots our sense of pity. We should enlarge our councils."

"You mean bring in more gods?"

"I think we need a human up here to teach us humanity."

"A man?"

"Or a woman. Someone who has lived on earth and known the toil and the danger and the suffering—and the hopes and the joys that people know."

"But who? Whom shall we call up here to teach us humanity?"

"I cannot tell you. If I were you, I should call upon the wisest of humankind and heed that opinion."

"Who is the wisest of humankind?"

"An old old man who has been blind for many years and in his blindness has seen more than anyone else. His name is Tyresias, but he is known simply as the Blind Man."

"You have given me much to think of, daughter. When the time comes, I shall consult with you again . . . and with your blind friend."

THE EARTH GIANT

GGGGGGGGGGGGGGGGGGGGGGGGGG

ONCE AGAIN, HERCULES HAD DONE WHAT HE SET OUT
to do and was sailing home with three golden apples.
Once again, he was sailing on a raft he had made himself with his spear as a mast and his lion skin as a sail.
The raft was slow and clumsy, but ever since his fight
with the octopus, he considered a raft to be the best
platform for fighting sea monsters, and that was more
important than speed.

However, he was not allowed to sail peacefully home.
Hera whispered to Poseidon, who called a half-gale out
of the north, driving the raft southward toward the hot
hump of land called Libya, where the giant Anteus
ruled. Hercules stood on his raft, studying the coast. He
didn't like what he saw. It was a bare scorched-looking
stretch of shore. But then he saw something he liked
even less. An enormous figure was wading toward him,
waist-deep in the sea.

"Can this be that giant Nereus spoke of?" wondered

Hercules. "The one I have to fight? I hope not. He's almost as big as Atlas."

He watched, horrified, as the giant reached into the water with a hand as big as a skiff and pulled out a swordfish. This was a terrible creature, as big as a shark; its sword was three feet long, and needle-pointed. But the giant cupped it out of the water like a boy catching a minnow and stood there, waves swirling around his waist, picking his teeth with the swordfish. He cast it back into the water, laughing a great rumbling laugh.

"Ho there," he called. "You, little one, standing on those twigs, who are you?"

"I am Hercules."

"I'm glad to see you, Hercules. You're bringing me three golden apples, aren't you?"

"I have three golden apples," said Hercules. "But not for you. One of them I must bring back to the king of Mycenae, for that is my task. Another one is a gift for a girl I know, named Iole. And the third is a gift for a young lady named Dienera."

"Very generous. But I'm afraid you don't understand. I am Anteus. This is my land and my harbor. And I am charging you a docking fee: three golden apples. You must pay or you cannot leave."

"I won't give you these apples. You'll have to take them."

"Do you really want me to use force? You're either very brave or very foolish or perhaps both. Don't you know that I can squash you like an ant?"

"Very well, I challenge you to a wrestling match. But let me come ashore and eat something and sleep a bit. I have sailed a long way."

"I like you, little Hercules," boomed Anteus. "You've

not only brought me three beautiful golden apples, but you're going to give me some sport as well. Come ashore, come ashore. We'll dine together. It'll be your last meal, of course, for tomorrow we fight."

When you're not used to the desert, it looks flat and ugly by day. But it can be beautiful at night. If you sleep outdoors, you see stars flaring like torches in a black sky, and they sink toward you, spinning like fire-wheels. You can weave their threads of light among your thoughts and make pictures that flicker against the velvet sky.

That's what Hercules was doing the night before the fight. He lay out on the sand looking up at the sky. He couldn't sleep. He was trying to puzzle out the verse spoken by Nereus. "To prove the giant's worth,/stretch him flat on earth." Earth was Mother Earth, Nereus had said. And contact with earth robbed Anteus of his strength. But was this the truth or a lie? Should he be-lieve it or do the opposite? Had the verse helped him before or not? A memory picture flared. He was stand-ing in the orchard throwing beehives into Ladon's gul-let. Had Nereus told him the truth about that? "Honey to the snake," he had said, but hadn't mentioned bees. Yet bees and honey were connected, very much so. So was that line a lie or not? And the next line, "Titan's burden take." Another picture flared, his own hunched shadow being crushed by the heavy rim of the sky. He had shouldered the Titan's burden and had almost been stuck with it forever. Yet, and this was true too, if he hadn't taken the sky from Atlas and frightened him by shaking the stars, he would never have been able to get the golden apples away from the orchard. So, were those lines true or not?

Now another picture flickered. Himself fighting the giant, Anteus, who was ten times his own size, strong enough to crush stones in his hands and to pick his teeth with swordfish. "To prove the giant's worth,/stretch him flat on earth." A truth or a lie or something between? Important to know, because when fighting an Anteus, one mistake is all you're allowed.

"Well, maybe it'll get clearer during the fight," he said to himself. "Best thing I can do now is get some sleep." So he chased the pictures and the puzzling verse out of his head, shut his eyes, and went fast asleep.

The next morning, they fought, and everyone in the land came to watch. They wrestled in a natural arena, a level place cupped by worn-down hills. The only rule in this match was that you had to come in without weapons. After the bout started, you could do anything you wanted, use anything you could get. Punching, kicking, gouging, choking—these were what the people wanted to see. But they were also used to being disappointed. No one had ever lasted more than a minute against Anteus.

The wrestlers stripped and oiled themselves. Slaves had to lean ladders against Anteus and climb with sponges and buckets of oil to the great plateau of his shoulders and the huge keg of his chest. The slaves departed. The wrestlers crouched.

"I barely reach to his kneecap," thought Hercules. "What can I possibly do? Well, when in doubt, charge!"

And the audience was amazed to see the man hurtle straight toward the giant. Anteus stood, waiting. Then he swung his leg in a terrific kick. His foot, traveling at enormous speed, hit the top of Hercules' head, which was hard as a rock. The small bones of instep and ankle

shattered like glass. Anteus hopped in agony. Hercules
thrust his shoulder against that leg, pushing it out from
under the giant, who went crashing to the ground. People sitting on the slopes felt the hills tremble as Anteus
fell full length on the ground, cracking his head on a
tree stump.

Hercules heard the ugly dry sound of that head splitting open. He saw the giant's blood soaking into the
ground, heard the rattling gasp of his breath. He stood
over his enemy, watching him die, and was amazed to
see the ashy face flush with life. He saw the giant's eyes
snap open, blazing with hatred, and the great chest
swell. Before he could dodge away, Anteus shot his arm
out, and the huge fingers caught Hercules by the throat
and began to strangle him.

The air darkened. The earth tilted. Hercules struggled, trying to tear those baling-hook fingers from his throat. In all his battles he had never felt a force equal to that of Anteus who, lying at ease on the ground, was calmly throttling Hercules to death with one hand. And, as his sight faded, he heard again the thin sneering voice of Nereus: "To prove the giant's worth,/stretch him flat on earth," and he knew suddenly the power of that lie. He knew that he should have done the opposite, for Anteus was the favorite son of Mother Earth and drew new strength from her touch. Felled to earth, the giant must rise again, stronger than before, and destroy the one who had laid him in his mother's lap.

This truth glimmered in the young man's darkening mind; it flared brightly, as truth does even when things are worst. And the strangling Hercules felt his tortured breathing ease a bit as the new idea cast a light that became strength beyond the strength of muscles.

He swung his arm in a desperate arc, knocking away the hand that was choking him. Taking a huge breath, he stooped swiftly, grasped the giant about the waist, and tried to pull him off the ground. But Anteus kicked and flailed and clung to the earth. And his mother, knowing he was in danger, pulled with all her strength—called gravity—trying to hug her son to her and keep him safe. Hercules couldn't pull him up, and he knew that if he couldn't, he was lost. He pulled and tugged. Anteus clung to the earth, which hugged him close.

"Father Zeus, help me now," whispered Hercules. And with those words, he felt the lightning energy that belonged to the Lord of the Sky fill his veins with a voltage of strength that allowed him to tear the struggling giant from the clutch of earth and lift him slowly toward the sky. His split head began to bleed again, and his life drained out as Hercules held him to the brassy sun.

Hercules kept holding the giant even after he was dead. He didn't dare let him touch earth again. He carried the enormous body to the beach and cast it into the sea and watched as the triangular fins of sharks began to cut the water.

THE SHIRT OF NESSUS

FRIGHTENING NEWS CAME TO THE KING: HERCULES had killed the Serpent of the Orchard and the giant Anteus; he had escaped Atlas and was coming to Mycenae with golden apples. The king was so terrified that he immediately climbed down into the pit that had been dug in his courtyard and hid there, shivering.

This time, Hercules refused to wait outside the walls. He knocked open the locked gate with one blow of his fist, marched into the courtyard, and tossed a golden apple into the pit. Leaving the city, he tore the gates from their hinges, twisted them into a tall spiral grille, and planted it outside the walls, where it became a roost for birds.

Then he went to see Dienera. But someone had gone before him into Calydon. His old enemy, Hera, realizing now that he could not be killed by force, had decided on treachery.

"He's never used the arrows he dipped into the

133

Hydra's blood," she said to herself. "Even when he desperately needed to kill some monster, he didn't take that easy way because he was afraid the poison might spread. Well, I'll see to it that he does use one, and I'll make sure the poison spreads—right through his own accursed body."

Now, there was a young warrior of Calydon, named Nessus, who was a marvelous horseman. He rode so well that his body seemed to grow out of the horse's body, and people called him "the centaur," for centaurs, remember, were half man, half horse. And Nessus loved Dienera and was very jealous of anyone who came near her. Hera walked into his sleep, and said, "Oh, Nessus, I am the goddess Hera. I have come to give you what you most want."

"Thank you, goddess. Dienera is what I most want. But she doesn't want me."

"If you do exactly as I say, she shall be your wife."

"But she says she's going to marry this Hercules. How I hate him!"

"Yes, he's hateful. You shall kill him and marry her."

"I'm a good fighter, goddess. And certainly no coward. But Hercules is supposed to be the strongest man in the world."

"He is still only a man, and I am a goddess. I intend to destroy him, and you shall be my helper. Your reward shall be Dienera."

"Tell me what to do."

"Hercules will visit her tomorrow. During his visit, they will quarrel, and she will run away from him, hoping that he will follow. But you will be hiding nearby. You will snatch her up into the saddle and gallop away."

"She'll never forgive me."

"Yes she will. She likes to be kidnapped. She'll be hoping that Hercules will rescue her. But when he doesn't show up, she'll be very angry at him and forgive you."

"Why won't he show up?"

"I'll see to it that he gets himself killed chasing you."

"Suppose he catches me first?"

"How can he? He'll be on foot, and you'll be on horseback. Besides, you're not afraid of a little risk, are you?"

"I'll be there tomorrow, goddess, on my fastest horse."

The next day, Hercules came to the castle and gave Dienera one of his golden apples. She was delighted. "Oh, thank you, thank you, thank you. Shall we get married today?"

"Not today, princess. I have to go somewhere."

"You just got here."

"I have a long way to go and must start."

"Where?'

"To find the girl who gets my third golden apple."

"You have another girl? Another apple? I want you to forget her and give it to me."

"I'm sorry, I can't do that."

"Who is this girl? Do you love her?"

"I guess so."

"More than you love me?"

"Well, it's different. She's still a child, I guess, but she's very brave and very clever. She saved my life twice. You'd like her if you knew her."

"I hate her! And I hate you too."

Blinded by tears, she ran away from him. She ran out

of the garden and into a field. Then ran more slowly and peeked over her shoulder to see if he was following. She felt a hand clutching her arm, felt herself being whisked into the air. Nessus had galloped out of a grove of trees where he had been hiding and snatched her into the saddle.

"Help!" she screamed. "Hercules! Help!"

Nessus galloped away. Hercules heard her scream and saw a horseman speeding away with her. He ran after the horse. Now, Nessus was riding a great raw-boned stallion that was the fastest horse in Calydon. Its flying hooves ate up the miles. Hercules ran with all his might. He saw that he was gaining, but too slowly. If the horseman meant to harm Dienera, he would have time before Hercules could catch him.

Hercules thought quickly. "The only way I can get him is with an arrow," he said to himself. "But it's a long way, and he's moving fast. I might hit her instead. I could kill the horse, but then they'd go flying off, and she might get hurt. I can't use an ordinary arrow; it will have to be a poison one. Then I can aim at his foot, and a scratch will stop him."

He knelt on the grass, searching in his quiver for a poison bolt. He notched the arrow. He pulled on the bowstring, drew it back, back, until the bow bent almost double, and let fly. The arrow cut through the air and grazed the rider's arm. Arm and shoulder immediately went blue. Poison ran through the man's veins. He stiffened and fell out of the saddle. The horse planted its feet, and stood there, trembling. Dienera slid off, bewildered. She looked down at her kidnapper. His face was blue. There was a bloody froth on his lips. His breath rattled in his throat.

136

"Dienera," he whispered, "I'm dying."

She dropped to her knees and looked into his face. Hera, who had planned all this, hovered invisibly over them. She whispered to the dying Nessus, "I'm sorry this happened. But I'll show you a way to avenge yourself on Hercules even after you're dead. If your poisoned blood can touch him, he will die too."

She kept whispering, telling Nessus exactly what to do. The dying man listened greedily. Dienera held him in her arms. She was sorry for him. She tried to cry, but couldn't quite. She did squeeze out a tear or two, which proved to her that she was really tenderhearted. And she shed a few more tears. They splashed on his face.

"Princess dear," whispered Nessus, "I'm sorry I kidnapped you. I know you'll marry Hercules, and I want to give you a wedding gift. Take my tunic and cut away the part that is stained with my blood. Weave that bloody cloth into a shirt you will make for Hercules. The heart blood of one who has loved you so well will be a magic potion. If Hercules wears that shirt, he can never love anyone but you."

"Thank you," said Dienera. "That's just what I need."

"Farewell, dear princess."

Nessus died. Dienera quickly tore away the bloody part of the garment and hid it in her tunic just before Hercules reached her. Hercules gazed down at the fallen horseman. He couldn't bear the look of him, lying there so blue-faced and rigid. He couldn't bear the thought that he had poisoned him.

"Go back to the castle," he said to Dienera. "I'll gather wood and make a fire and burn his body, so that

138

his blood won't soak into the ground and poison the grass. I'll come to you when I'm finished."

Dienera returned to the castle. She went to a loom and wove a shirt for Hercules. She had never woven anything before; she had left that to her slaves. But now Hera hovered invisibly, guiding her hands. And the shirt she wove was a gorgeous thing, decorated with pictures of the battles fought by Hercules . . . the Nemean Lion, the Hydra, Anteus . . . pictures of all his adventures woven into the shirt with colored threads. In the very middle of its back, she inserted the patch that was taken from the shirt of Nessus and steeped in poison blood. Hera kept helping her, and her fingers flew with magical speed. She was finished by the time Hercules returned to the castle. She went to him and said:

"Hercules, dear, I'm sorry I was so mean before. But I won't be jealous, I swear. Go have a nice visit with Iole. And to show that you love me too, take this shirt that I have woven and promise me that you'll wear it when you see her—so that I'll know you're thinking of me."

"Thank you," said Hercules. "I'll wear it with pleasure."

Hercules ran along the shore toward the driftwood shack where Iole lived with the Blind Man. Iole, with her keen eyes, spotted him while he was still a long way off. She ran to meet him. It was a sunny day, too hot for a heavy embroidered shirt, but Hercules had promised Dienera that he would be wearing it when he met Iole, so he had put it on.

He was so eager to see Iole that he was running fast and was hotter than ever, so hot that the clot of Hydra blood began to melt, and the wet shirt clung to his back. The girl came running to him and leaped into his arms. He set her on his shoulders, and gave her a golden apple. She rode his shoulders, laughing with joy, and tossing the apple into the air.

"Why are you wearing this tapestry?" she said. "Some girl made it for you—that weepy princess, I'll bet."

She heard a curious gasping sound and thought he was laughing. She felt him stagger and just managed to slide off his shoulders before he fell. She thought he had stumbled. He climbed to his feet and stood there swaying.

The Blind Man came limping up. "Greetings, Hercules," he said.

Hercules didn't answer. He couldn't answer. He tried to speak, but no words came. Iole screamed as she saw his face turning blue. The Hydra venom melted the inside of the shirt, turning each of its fibers into a thorn, which pierced his back and shoulders. The thorns wove themselves into the fibers of his flesh, fusing them into one mat of nettles. He felt himself scorching. The pain was worse than anything he had ever known. It burned through his flesh, into his marrow. For the first time in his life, he screamed.

Iole saw his face twist in agony, saw his hands lift and claw his face. She saw those hands grasping the shirt at the shoulders, trying to tear it off. The shirt stuck. It was part of his skin now. Hercules pulled at the shirt. He pulled with all his might, and tore the shirt off his back, tearing his own flesh away, peeling himself to the bone.

Pain killed him before the poison could reach his

heart. His legs folded. He fell in a puddle of hissing blood. Iole's face was white as bone. With him gone, she didn't want to stay in the world for one second. She knelt to him and kissed his lips, drinking the poison froth, and fell dead with her head on his chest.

Tyresias raised his blind face to the sky and howled like a wolf. "O Zeus," he cried. "Father Zeus, hear me now, I pray. Hear me as I bear witness to this man, the best of his kind. He killed a monster once, and that monster was the Hydra. He cut off a hundred dragon heads and buried them under rocks, for they kept snapping after death. And each of those poison heads became a stream. The streams mingled and became a river, the river Hydra, clear and pure, and very beautiful in the tumbling of its waters. For in your wisdom, O Zeus, you have made the earth use everything it is given, even monstrous matter. So now I call upon you, O mighty and mysterious one, whose shadow is justice, and ask that the same Hydra blood which this man's courage made into a river of singing waters, that this same poison running in his body now, shall run pure again, restoring him to the wholeness of his flesh."

Zeus stood with Athena on Olympus. She had heard the Blind Man howling and had made her father listen. The words of the prophet drifted up to Zeus and made him frown.

"Hera has done this deed," he said. "I forbade her to kill him herself, but she has done it through trickery."

"Behold the man," said Athena. "He, lying there, was the best and strongest, the bravest and most gentle of humankind. Let him join us here on Olympus and teach us to be human, too, before man, learning cruelty from us, destroys himself."

"So be it," said Zeus.

Far below, on the shore of the flashing sea, Hercules arose. He was clothed in flesh again, all new, milky and lustrous. His face was like the evening star, streaming light. He stood taller than before, changed, joyous, god-like.

He called. A chariot coasted down the steeps of air, drawn by twelve golden eagles, and the chariot was golden too. He lifted Iole into the chariot. And the gold of the eagles and the gold of the chariot flying straight toward the sun made so hot a stream of golden light that it pierced the old man's blindness. His sight was restored, and the first thing he saw after forty years of darkness was the golden chariot streaking away, and Hercules holding Iole in his arms.

So Hercules was taken among the gods and lived among them, teaching them humanity. And Hera pretended it was all her idea.

There are different stories about what happened to Iole. Some say she became a goddess, that her name was shortened to Eos, and that she rode in the sun chariot, painting the dawn. Some say that Hercules drove that sun chariot, and that his name was changed to Helios. Others say, though, that Athena simply changed the girl into a gull, who flies forever over the sea, crying "Hercules, Hercules . . ."

We do know, though, what happened to the shirt. It fell into the hands of Hestia, Goddess of the Hearth, who washed its poison away and cut out its embroidered pictures. From time to time, she takes a handful of these pictures and visits her hearths, scattering them among the flames, so that boys and girls, dreaming into the fire, see pictures in the heart of the flame and pin their own face on Hercules as he fights the Nemean Lion and the Hydra and the three-bodied giant . . . as he wrestles the river in all its changes and ties the octopus into knots and throws Anteus and does all those other brave and wonderful things. And these boys and girls, dreaming into the fire, promise themselves that they will be brave when they grow up and always fight those shapes of evil called monsters and always dare to be gentle, too.

About the Author

BERNARD EVSLIN has been a playwright, film writer, and director. His plays have been produced both on and off Broadway. He is the author of a novel about his Hollywood experiences as well as several books for young readers, including *Heroes, Gods and Monsters of the Greek Myths; Signs and Wonders: Tales from the Old Testament;* and *The Green Hero: Early Adventures of Finn McCool,* which was nominated for a National Book Award in Children's Literature. Mr. Evslin lives in New Rochelle, New York.

About the Illustrator

JOS. A. SMITH studied at the Pennsylvania Academy of Fine Arts and at the Pratt Institute in New York, where he has been a member of the faculty for over twenty years. In the course of his career there have been numerous exhibitions of his paintings, drawings and sculpture, and his political cartoons have appeared in such magazines as *Time* and *Newsweek*.